STUDY GUIDE

to accompany

Robin Wolf

MARRIAGES AND FAMILIES IN A DIVERSE SOCIETY

Laurence A. Basirico
Elon College

Study Guide to accompany Wolf, MARRIAGES AND FAMILIES IN A DIVERSE SOCIETY

ISBN: 0-065-02013-8

95 96 97 98 99 9 8 7 6 5 4 3 2 1

CONTENTS

Preface

To the Student

This study guide is intended to accompany Robin Wolf's MARRIAGES AND FAMILIES. It is not intended to, nor will it, serve as a substitute for Robin Wolf's text. Properly used in conjunction with Wolf's text, this guide will help you understand the text material better and help prepare you for exams.

There are six parts to each chapter of this guide: a chapter outline, chapter learning objectives, key points for review, key terms, a practice test, and projects. Below, you will find a description of each part and suggestions how to use them.

Chapter Outline
The chapter outline is identical to the one found at the beginning of each chapter in Wolf's text. It is included here to help prepare you for what the chapter is about before you read it and to refresh your memory of what the chapter is about after you have read it. After reading Wolf's text carefully, you should have a general idea as to what each of these sections in the outline is about. After you have read the complete chapter in the text, if there is something on the outline that you are not familiar with or do not remember, it would be a good idea to re-read that section in the text.

Chapter Learning Objectives
The chapter learning objectives list the major ideas in each chapter that Wolf is trying to get across. Read over the objectives before you begin reading the chapter in the text. These objectives should be used as a guide to help you focus your attention as you study the chapter. Read over the chapter objectives periodically as you are reading the chapter in order to help keep you focused on what you should be learning from the chapter. When you finish reading and studying the chapter in Wolf's text, use the chapter learning objectives as practice essay questions. Each of the objectives has been written in such a way as to act as an essay or discussion question.

Key Points for Review
The key points for review summarize some of the major ideas, theories, concepts, and research findings discussed in the respective chapters in Wolf's text. The key points have been designed to help you recall some of the major topics and to help refresh your memory about the material found in the chapter. They should not be used a substitute for reading and studying the text but, instead, as summary review of the material. You will not be able to answer satisfactorily the practice test, the learning objectives, or the projects without thoroughly reading the appropriate chapter in the text first.

Key Terms
The key terms are found in the respective chapter in Wolf's textbook. In this study guide, each key term is listed followed by a page number in parentheses indicating where it is discussed in the textbook. Find each term, briefly define or explain it in the space provided, include an example that will help you remember it, and include any other comments from class or the text that may help you explain the term.

Practice Test
Each practice test consists of twenty to thirty multiple-choice questions. You should be able to answer these questions satisfactorily after studying the respective chapter in the text and after using the first four parts of the study guide material in each chapter. The answers to the practice questions are found at the end of the study guide. These questions have been written independently of the instructor's test manual, so simply memorizing the answers to them will not serve as adequate preparation for examinations that you take in class. You should use the practice tests and the answer key to help you study and review the key ideas found in the chapters. As you go through your results, make sure that you understand why each of the answers is correct or incorrect.

In addition to the multiple choice questions, you should use the chapter objectives as practice essay questions. Each objective has been formulated to be used as possible essay or discussion questions.

Projects
At the end of each chapter you will find one or more projects that deal with some aspects or themes found within the chapter. Each project is divided into four sections: a journal activity, an essay, a bibliography, and a research paper. Each project can be assigned in its entirety, or specific parts of the project can be assigned. The projects have been designed in such a way as to take you through various levels of thought or research about a topic in stages. Each project, in its entirety, is an example of how a research project can be carried out in stages that build upon each other. Each stage is described below.

The journal part of each project is usually an exercise in conducting some field work (observation or interviews) and/or reflecting about a particular topic related to marriages and families. The field work journal is usually the beginning stage—and a very important part—of any social science research. The journal part of each project has been designed to give you direct, hands-on experience in conducting research and to give you the opportunity to reflect on important themes regarding marriages and families. The material you accumulate in your field work journal portion of the project will be used as the basis for the other parts of the project.

The essay option within each project usually asks you to discuss and analyze the material that you accumulated in the journal portion of the project. There are three purposes of the essay activities: 1) to have you apply some of the theories and concepts found within the related chapter in the text to the material that you collected in your field work journal; 2) to have you discuss, analyze, and summarize the material you collected in your journal, and to have you develop a first draft of the research paper, should you have it assigned to you.

The bibliography option usually requires that you develop a bibliography of articles and/or books written by social scientists about the theme that you explored in the field work journal. The bibliography serves as a source of material that you can use should you be required to complete the research paper portion of the project.

The research paper option usually asks that you integrate material from your field work journal, your essay, and your bibliography to discuss a particular theme in depth. The purpose of this portion of the project is to have you integrate the ideas, theories, and conclusions of social scientists who have conducted research on the topic with the ideas and conclusions you have reached in your observations and analysis of the topic.

To the Instructor

Please read the above message to the students. It describes the parts to this study guide and the purposes of each part. A couple of items are particularly important and bear repeating to you.

First, the study guide is intended to be used as a supplement to the text and not a substitute. The students will neither obtain all of the material presented in the text nor a thorough discussion of the material that is included for discussion. However, if used appropriately, this study guide will serve as an invaluable source to help students understand and retain the text material.

Second, the learning objectives that are listed in each chapter have been designed to serve also as discussion or essay questions for examinations. Most can be used verbatim for examination questions.

Third, the projects at the end of each chapter of this study guide have been designed to have students complete research projects in stages or to have the students complete only one portion of the project. Any or all of the activities of a project can be assigned. Obviously, the projects are too extensive to require that students complete all the stages of more than a few of these. There are many ways in which to use the projects. Once you become familiar with the way in which they are organized you will probably develop your own methods of using them in your course. In the meantime, here are a few suggestions. I have used each of the following approaches in different classes that I teach using projects that I design for each course and each works very well.

- Require students to complete one (or more) of each type of assignment (for example, one journal, one essay, one bibliography, and one research paper) on different topics that you choose.
- Require students to keep an overall journal for the semester and have them complete one journal activity from a project for each chapter of the text that you assign. If that is too much work for one semester, you might have them select a reasonable number to complete by the end of the semester.
- Require students to complete all of the options for one project—from field work journal to essay to bibliography to final research paper.
- Modify the projects to reflect a particular concern you might have or something you are emphasizing in class.

• Modify the requirements of the projects. The page length, number of bibliographic sources, observation time, and so on have been included as suggestions. Consider the needs of your course and the level of your students as you make your assignments.

On the following page I have included an example of an evaluation form that I generally use to provide feedback to students for different activities from the projects that they do in my classes.

This study guide has been written with the goal of making the study of marriages and families more understandable and accessible to students. I hope that you and your students find this study guide useful and are able to integrate it as a meaningful part of your course. I appreciate any comments or suggestions you may have for future editions. Please send them to me at the Department of Sociology, Elon College, Elon College, North Carolina 27244 or send them via e-mail to: basirico@vax1.elon.edu.

—Laurence A. Basirico

Name____

Project #_____________

Type _____journal _____essay_____bibliography _____research paper

1. Was assignment turned in on time?

Yes_____ No_____ Days late______

2. Did student follow all instructions completely and correctly?

1 2 3 4 5

Comment:

3. Was student conscientious in completing assignment? Did student put in sufficient time and thought relevant to the assignment?

1 2 3 4 5

Comment:

4. Does the student correctly understand the social science ideas, perspectives, concepts, or theories on which the assignment is based?

1 2 3 4 5

Comment:

5. Does the student follow a format appropriate to the assignment?

1 2 3 4 5

Comment:

6. Is correct spelling and proper grammar used throughout the student's work?

1 2 3 4 5

Comment:

7. Is the level of depth of analysis, exploration, or discussion appropriate to the assignment?

1 2 3 4 5

Comment:

8. Is the length of the completed work appropriate for the assignment?

1 2 3 4 5

Comment:

Grade:__________

Comment:

CHAPTER 1

PERSPECTIVES ON THE FAMILY

CHAPTER OUTLINE

What is a Family?
- Traditional Definition of the Family
- U.S. Bureau of the Census Definition of the Family
- Revisionist Definition of the Family
- Defining the Family in this Book

What is Marriage?
- Monogamy
- Polyandry
- Polygyny
- Group Marriage

Is the Family in a State of Decline
- Family Decline Perspective: The Family in a State of Decline
- Family Change Perspective: Strength in Diversity

Divorce
- Family Decline Perspective: The Family in a State of Decline
- Family Change Perspective: Strength in Diversity

Married Women and Employment
- Family Decline Perspective: The Family in a State of Decline
- Family Change Perspective: Strength in Diversity

Cohabitation
- Family Decline Perspective: The Family in a State of Decline
- Family Change Perspective: Strength in Diversity

Explaining Demographic Trends
- The Post-Industrial Family After 1960
- Was There a Golden Age?
- Harbor Not Haven

Structural Diversity Among Families

One-Parent Families

Stepfamilies

Two-Earner Families

Families Which Include Extended Kin

Cultural Diversity Among Families

Biculturalism

CHAPTER LEARNING OBJECTIVES

After studying this chapter, you should be able to:

- define, discuss, critique and understand the different definitions of "the family;"
- understand the importance of being able to distinguish between definitions of "the family;"
- define and discuss various forms of marriage and how they are relative to cultures in which they are found;
- objectively examine the various positions about the health or decline of the American family;
- discuss the trends of labor force participation of women and men and how they affect and are affected by the changing family;
- identify and discuss demographic trends relevant to the family and why they have occurred;
- discuss the ways in which families are structurally diversified and why;
- discuss the ways in which families are culturally diversified.

KEY POINTS FOR REVIEW

- The American family is changing. Reasons for the change include the high divorce rate, the rise in cohabitation, delayed marriage, evolving sexual patterns, changing gender roles, the AIDS crisis, changes in dating patterns, and others. This book examines the family as a changing institution, its diverse forms, and how it is related to diverse structural and cultural factors.

• Because the family has undergone many changes, a debate about the definition of the family has emerged. The "traditionalist" approach defines families as being formed through childbearing and says the central core of the family is a parent-child relationship. The "census" approach—for the purposes of collective census data on families—defines the family as two or more people related by blood, marriage, or adoption who share a common residence. The "family change" approach provides a broader definition of the family to include partnerships based on a long-term intimate sexual relationship. There are important criticisms of each of these approaches. Wolf's definition is that families consist of two or more people related through blood, marriage, adoption, legal custody or an ongoing sexual relationship, who share a common residence.

• While family remains a difficult concept to define sociologically, defining marriage is less problematic. Wolf defines marriage as a sexual relationship between two adults who cooperate economically, which is marked by a ceremony or ritual that is publicly recognized as changing the social status of the partners involved. There are four basic forms of marriage: monogamy (one husband and one wife), polyandry (one wife and two or more husbands), polygyny (one husband and two or more wives), and group marriage (two or more husbands and two or more wives). The type of marriage that exists within a society is related to the cultural and economic conditions of that society.

• Social changes related to the American family—such as the rise in the divorce rate, the sexual revolution, the growth of single-parent families and the employment of mothers—have led to discussions about the state of health of the family. There are two broad perspectives about the health of the American family. The family decline perspective—that the family is in a state of decline—holds that the family is under siege as it is battered by the aforementioned changes. The family change perspective—that the diversity of families is a sign of the strength and resilience of the institution—holds that the family is not crumbling, but instead becoming more complex and diverse.

• Demographic trends can also be interpreted from the family decline and family change perspectives. Viewing the high divorce rate, the family decline perspective argues that the United States has become a high-divorce-rate society and people have a weakened commitment to marriage. Additionally, the family decline perspective says that divorce has a negative impact on children. Thus, divorce is interpreted as a sign of family decline. The family change perspective claims that divorce often ends unacceptable relationships and creates a "new beginning." This position maintains that it is not divorce itself which has the negative impact on children, but the negative impact is the result of the marital conflict both before and after the divorce. From this view, divorce and remarriage are viewed as evidence that Americans highly value marriage and are unwilling to accept marital and family relationships that are unsatisfying or detrimental.

• The labor force participation rate among married women has doubled since 1960. The typical family today is the two-earner family. The family decline perspective argues that since the function of the family is to raise the next generation of children, the increase in two-earner families should be looked at with alarm. From this view, children will increasingly be cared for by people other than their parents, thus leading to insecure attachments and other associated problems. By contrast, the family change perspective is that the increased labor force participation of women is a sign of increasing stability in families resulting from shared household, child-rearing, and breadwinning responsibilities between husbands and wives.

• Today, almost half of all people who enter first marriages have previously cohabited. The family decline perspective argues that this trend suggests that the willingness to form committed relationships is declining and Americans are rejecting family life. By contrast, the family change perspective argues that the rise of cohabitation should not be viewed as a sign that Americans are rejecting family, but an alternative to marriage for people who are not yet in a position to marry.

• All industrialized societies—with the exception of Japan—have undergone significant demographic changes since the 1960s, such as a rise in the divorce rate, increase in the employment of married women, and growing cohabitation. These family changes have stemmed primarily from changes from industrial society to post-industrial society, rather than changes in personal attitude. With the change to a post-industrial society, there has been a demand in well-paid jobs for increased education and skill. The increased education and skills for men and women has enabled more women to enter the labor force and has made divorce possible for a greater number of people as men and women became less dependent upon each other. Other changes have included the sexual revolution, delayed marriage, a decline in fertility and increase in life expectancy.

• Families in American society are becoming increasingly diverse, both structurally and culturally. One-parent families, step-families, two-earner families, extended families, subfamilies, bicultural families, as well as traditional families, exist. It is important to view families from the perspective of those who experience them in order to create fair social policies that pertain to families.

KEY TERMS

The following key terms are found in your textbook on the page number indicated in parentheses. In the space provided, write a brief definition of the key term. Then provide an example of the term, such as a culture in which the practice takes place, or people that you might know whose behavior illustrates the term. You could include issues that you might have read about in the news or in a book, or anything else that will illustrate the term and help you remember it. Include any comments from your class discussions or textbook that might help you remember and understand these key terms.

family (p. 9)

marriage (p. 9)

monogamy (p. 10)

serial monogamy (p. 10)

polyandry (p. 10)

ideal marriage (p. 10)

polygyny (p. 11)

group marriage (p. 11)

fraternal polyandry (p. 12)

patrilocal residence (p. 12)

demographic trends (p. 13)

high-divorce-rate society (p. 14)

labor force (p. 16)

cohabitation (p. 19)

industrial society (p. 20)

post-industrial society (p. 20)

family wage (p. 20)

global economy (p. 20)

sexual revolution (p. 21)

independent living (p. 21)

nuclear family (p. 25)

extended family (p. 25)

subfamilies (p. 26)

biculturalism (p. 27)

PRACTICE TEST

Multiple Choice

1. According to sociologists, the most basic form of social organization is:
   a) the clique
   b) the church
   c) the family
   d) the military

2. According to the Gallup Poll, what percentage of married people in the United States are "very satisfied" with their marriages?
   a) 100%
   b) 85%
   c) 50%
   d) 20%

3. The definition of the family that holds that families are formed through childbearing and that the central core of the family is a parent-child relationship linking two generations through adoption or birth is:
   a) the traditional definition of the family
   b) the U. S. Bureau of the Census definition of the family
   c) the social change definition of the family
   d) the statistical definition of the family

4. The definition of the family that stresses the that the quality of the relationship, not its legal standing, is the key criteria in determining whether or not a couple qualifies as a family is:
   a) the traditional definition of the family
   b) the U. S. Bureau of the Census definition of the family
   c) the social change definition of the family
   d) the statistical definition of the family

5. The definition of the family that says a family includes two or more people related by blood, marriage, adoption, legal custody or an ongoing sexual relationship who share a common residence is:
   a) the traditional definition of the family
   b) the U. S. Bureau of the Census definition of the family
   c) the social change definition of the family
   d) more applicable for social science research than any of the above perspectives

6. A criticism of the traditional definition of the family is that:
   a) it is difficult to quantitatively conduct research based on such a rigid definition
   b) it excludes much of the diversity and complexity of modern families
   c) it defines cohabiting couples as a family
   d) defining the family in terms of the quality of the relationship could make it difficult to conduct research on the family

7. A criticism of the revisionist definition of the family is that:
   a) it is difficult to quantitatively conduct research based on such a rigid definition
   b) it excludes much of the diversity and complexity of modern families
   c) it excludes cohabiting couples and thus represents a form of bias against low income couples and divorced persons
   d) defining the family in terms of the quality of the relationship could make it difficult to conduct research on the family

8. Which of the following terms refers to the marriage of one wife to two or more husbands:
   a) serial monogamy
   b) group marriage
   c) polygyny
   d) polyandry

9. According to the family decline perspective, which of the following supports the view that the family in the U.S. is in a state of decline?
   a) the rise in the divorce rate
   b) the growth of single-parent families
   c) the increased employment of mothers outside the home
   d) all of the above

10. Which view best represents the social change perspective on the state of the family in the U.S.?
    a) recent demographic trends indicate that the family is changing, not breaking down
    b) high divorce rates and rates of remarriage do not indicate a state of family decline but, rather that people still highly value families
    c) there are no negative effects of being a high-divorce-rate society
    d) a and b above

11. The typical family in the U.S. today:
    a) undergoes a divorce
    b) is a two-earner family
    c) is bicultural
    d) earns above $70,000 per year

12. Since 1960, the labor force participation rate among married women:
   a) has doubled
   b) has tripled
   c) has declined some
   d) has remained about the same

13. Since 1960, the labor force participation rate among married men:
   a) has doubled
   b) has tripled
   c) has declined some
   d) has remained about the same

14. Since 1970, the number of people in the United States entering first time marriages who have had experience with cohabitation has:
   a) doubled
   b) quadrupled
   c) stayed around the same
   d) declined

15. Since the 1960s, all industrialized nations have experienced a rise in the divorce rate, an increase in the employment of married women, and growing cohabitation with the exception of:
   a) the United States
   b) Sweden
   c) England
   d) Japan

16. Which of the following best describes post-industrial families:
   a) urban families that are shaped by the societal need for higher education and career development in both men and women
   b) urban families that are shaped by the societal need for factory-produced goods
   c) suburban families that are shaped by the societal need for increased food supply
   d) rural families that are shaped by the societal need for increased food supply

17. Which of the following was not a factor that impacted American families at the time the United States was entering the post-industrial era after 1960:
   a) delayed marriage
   b) the sexual revolution
   c) a decline in the divorce rate
   d) life-cycle changes

18. In terms of diversity, American families are:
    a) becoming increasingly diverse in their structure and organization
    b) becoming increasingly similar to one another in their structure and organization
    c) are, when demographics are taken into consideration, not really that different than a generation ago
    d) none of the above

19. Over the last two decades, the number of one-parent families headed by fathers has:
    a) declined by 50%
    b) tripled
    c) doubled
    d) has remained about the same

20. The typical married couple today:
    a) has the husband as the prime breadwinner and the wife as a homemaker
    b) forms a two-earner family
    c) has the wife as the prime breadwinner
    d) none of the above

NOTES:

PROJECTS

PROJECT 1.1 Social Policies, Social Issues and the Definition of Family

As discussed in this chapter, various approaches to defining the family have emerged. The "traditionalist" approach defines families as being formed through childbearing and says the central core of the family is a parent-child relationship. The "census" approach defines the family as two or more people related by blood, marriage, or adoption who share a common residence. The "social change" approach provides a broader definition of the family to include partnerships based on a long-term intimate sexual relationship. The definition used by Wolf in this book is that families consist of two or more people related through blood, marriage, adoption, legal custody or an ongoing sexual relationship who share a common residence. The various definitions of the family are of more than academic interest. Often, policies and issues emerge that are dependent upon how family is defined.

Journal instructions:

1. Re-read the sections of the chapter in which the various definitions of the family are discussed. List the important characteristics of each definition in your journal.

2. Look through back editions of newspapers and newsmagazines (such as *The New York Times, Los Angeles Times, Washington Post, Time Magazine, Newsweek,* and so on) for the past six months and identify policy controversies or debates that would affect families (for example, family leave, day care, health care, divorce, and so on). Try to find at least six policies and/or issues and list them in your journal.

3. Discuss how using each of the definitions of family might lead to different positions or opinions about the policy.

4. Try to find news articles that illustrate or imply each of the various definitions of the family.

Option: essay

Using the information that you compiled in your journal, write an essay (around three to four pages, typed) in which you discuss the relevance of the definitions of the family for social policies. That is, discuss and illustrate how the definition of family can determine and lead to debate about the types of social policies that should be created to deal with the issues.

Option: bibliography

Select one of the policies that you wrote about in your journal. Using your library's indexes, develop a bibliography of ten to fifteen articles from the popular literature (newspapers, news magazines, commentary magazines, and so on) and from the social science literature (sociology journals) about the policy or issue you selected. Be sure to have a good balance between social science journal articles and popular articles. Type your bibliography using the bibliographic style found in your textbook.

Option: research paper
Complete the above journal and bibliographic instructions if you have not already done so. Write a paper (around five to seven pages, typed) in which you:

1. Introduce the policy debate or controversial issue and discuss what the various positions are.

2. Discuss the policy debate or issue from the perspective of each of the definitions of family offered in this chapter.

3. Integrate material from your bibliography (both popular and sociological literature) that you have found that illustrates the perspectives of the respective definitions of family.

4. Select one position and use material from this chapter and the sociology journals to support it.

5. Provide proper documentation of your references throughout the paper and include a reference page.

PROJECT 1.2 The Family in Health or Decline

Social changes related to the American family—such as the rise in the divorce rate, the sexual revolution, the growth of single-parent families and the employment of mothers—have led to discussions about the health of the family. There are two broad perspectives about the health of the American family. The family decline perspective—that the family is in a state of decline—holds that the family is under siege as it is battered by the aforementioned changes. The family change perspective—that the diversity of families is a sign of the strength and resilience of the institution—holds that the family is not crumbling, but instead becoming more complex and diverse.

Journal instructions:
1. In your college or public library, locate copies of the most recent national, state, or local census, if they are available. If they are not available, look for the *Statistical Abstract of the United States*. If none of these materials are available, you can complete this project using the graphs presented in Chapter 1 of your textbook.

2. Examine each census and make a list in your journal of all of the types of data that are available about families. The list is extensive and contains things such as head of household, number of children, income, divorce rates, and so on.

3. Select five types of data that you think are indicators of the state of the American family (for example, divorce rate, number of children, and so on). Use these five items to compare families in the nation, your state, and your city in 1990, 1980, 1970, and if available, 1960. For example, what was the divorce rate in the nation, your state, and your city in 1990, 1980, 1970 and 1960? How many female-headed households were there in 1990, 1980, 1970 and 1960? And so on. Compile the rates for these indicators, in table form, and summarize in your own words the results of your findings.

4. Interview five people whose occupation leads them to deal with family issues or is knowledgeable about issues related to the family (for example, minister, lawyer, therapist, mediator, sociology professor, insurance agent, politician, and so on). Present them with the results of your census findings—or some of the graphs in Chapter 1 of the textbook, such as the graph showing the rise in the divorce rate—and ask them to comment on the state of the family in the United States today. Record their comments in your journal.

5. Look through newspapers and magazines from the past few months for editorials and letters to the editor reflecting on the state of the family in American society.

Option: essay

Use the information that you collected in your journal (above) and discussions from your text to write an essay (three to five pages, typed) reflecting on the state of health or decline of the family in American society today. Be sure to integrate your census findings, interviews, news editorials, and ideas from your text in your discussion. Is their more than one interpretation of the data? How might the data be interpreted differently? Discuss and support your views.

Option: bibliography

Use your library's indexes (for example, *Social Science Index, Sociological Abstracts*, or other journal indexes) to develop a bibliography of ten to fifteen sociology articles that discuss demographic trends related to the issues for which you collected census data. Type your bibliography using the bibliographic style found in your textbook or in the sociology articles.

Option: research paper

If you have not done so already, complete the above journal, essay and bibliography instructions. Write a paper (around seven pages, typed) in which you discuss the state of health and/or decline of the family in American society today. In your paper, be sure to:

1. Cite and discuss the demographic trends that you identified from the census.

2. Discuss the various positions that can be taken about the state of the family. (INSTRUCTIONS CONTINUED ON NEXT PAGE)

3. Use your interview material and editorials to discuss some views about the health of the family that are commonly held.

4. Integrate material from five of the sociology articles and your own above research that you compiled for your journal and provide a balanced discussion of the state of the family in American society today. Provide proper documentation of your references throughout the paper and include a reference page.

NOTES:

PROJECT 1.3 Experiencing Family Diversity

One of the key points of this chapter is that families in American society are becoming increasingly diverse, both structurally and culturally. One-parent families, step-families, two-earner families, extended families, subfamilies, bicultural families, as well as traditional families, exist. Families do not exist in a vacuum but are affected by the sociocultural forces in which they exist. There are many structural patterns around which families are organized and these depend upon the culture. These patterns pertain to norms for choice of marriage partner, number of marriage partners, residence, descent and inheritance, authority, child-rearing practices, and so on. It is important to view families from the perspective of those who experience them in order to create fair social policies that pertain to families.

Journal instructions:

1. Look through this chapter and at the outlines for each of the other chapters in your textbook. In your journal, identify and define the various structural patterns around which families may be organized and briefly describe the possible variations of each pattern.

2. Describe the structural patterns around which your family of orientation (the family in which you were raised) is organized.

3. Identify a person you know whose family of orientation is structured differently from yours. For example, if you are from a family where there is a male head of household who is the prime breadwinner and a female who is a full time homemaker, you might find a person who lives within a family headed by a single mother. There are numerous possibilities. Try to identify someone whose family is extremely different from yours. From the person you identified, obtain information about the various structural patterns around which his or her family is organized. Ask the person to explain why these patterns make sense within his or her family.

4. Spend four or five hours with the person you identified and his or her family. If this is not possible, try to have the person you identified spend a few hours with you and discuss, in detail, what life is like in his or her family. Afterwards, reflect and write about your views about this person's family and the way that it operates and compare it with the views you held about this type of family before you learned about it from your friend. Have your judgments about this type of family changed? Do the behaviors that you learned about make sense within the context of that family?

5. Identify four occupations in which knowledge of structural and cultural diversity within families may be useful. List these in your journal and briefly discuss how/why this knowledge would be useful in these occupations.

Option: essay
Use your journal notes to write an essay (around three to five pages, typed) in which you compare your family of orientation with the type of family that you identified above.

Option: bibliography
Complete the above journal instructions. Then, through library research, compile a bibliography of ten to fifteen sociology articles and/or books (excluding textbooks) about the type of family that you learned about in your journal activity. For example, if the person you identified is from a single female-headed household, then compile a bibliography of articles about single female-headed households. Type your bibliography following the format used in your textbook or found in the sociology articles.

Option: research paper
If you have not already done so, complete the above journal and bibliography activities. Write a paper (around five to seven pages, typed) in which you use your journal and four or five articles from your bibliography to compare and discuss the way your family is organized with the way that the type of family you identified above is organized. In your paper, include a discussion of why and how this knowledge is useful within different occupations. Provide proper documentation of your references throughout the paper and include a reference page.

CHAPTER 2

RESEARCH METHODS AND SOCIAL THEORIES

CHAPTER OUTLINE

The Scientific Method

Aiming for Accuracy
- Validity
- Reliability

Methods of Collecting Data
- Surveys
- Experiments
- Demography

What is a Social Theory?

Structural Functional Theory
- Application: The Old Order Amish
- Critique of Structural Functional Theory

Conflict Theory
- Application: Social Class and the Definition of the Family
- Critique of Conflict Theory

Exchange Theory
- Application: Lower Class African American Families
- Critique of Exchange Theory

Systems Theory
- Application: Families with an Alcoholic Parent
- Critique of Systems Theory

CHAPTER LEARNING OBJECTIVES

After studying this chapter, you should be able to:

- discuss some of the possible pitfalls in conducting social research about the family;

- identify, understand and discuss each of the stages of the scientific method;

- identify and discuss four methods of collecting data and the advantages and disadvantages of each when conducting research on issues pertaining to the family;

- explain the difference between validity and reliability and be able to identify whether or not survey questions are valid and reliable;

- explain structural-functional theory, apply it to the study of the family and critique it;

- explain conflict theory, apply it to the study of the family and critique it;

- explain exchange theory, apply it to the study of the family and critique it;

- explain systems theory, apply it to the study of the family and critique it;

KEY POINTS FOR REVIEW

• In order for research about the family to produce accurate results, social scientists use the scientific method. The steps of the scientific method include the following: formulating a research question, specifying the independent and dependent variables, developing a hypothesis, operationalizing the variables, selecting a population to study, selecting a sample, collecting the data, and analyzing the results.

• It is generally impossible and impractical for researchers to interview or observe the entire population that they want to study. Therefore, a sample of the population is selected to interview or observe. However, the accuracy of the results of the research very much depend upon how representative the sample is of the population under study. The best way to achieve a representative sample of the population under study is to obtain a random sample of the population, giving each person in the population an equal chance of being interviewed or observed. When reporting the results of the research, it is essential that the researcher explain how the sample was obtained so that the results may be interpreted accordingly.

• Correlation does not necessarily mean causation. This means that even though a strong association exists between an independent variable and a dependent variable, the independent variable is not necessarily the cause of the dependent variable. This is called a spurious relationship. For example, a positive correlation between virginity at marriage (the independent variable) and a low divorce rate (the dependent variable) does not necessarily mean that being a virgin at marriage leads to low divorce rate. Virgins may be more likely to have traditional values, and it may be the traditional values that lead to a lower divorce rate. Nevertheless, if there is a strong correlation (association) between the independent variable and the dependent variable—even though it may be a spurious relationship—the independent variable is still a good predictor of the dependent variable.

• Researchers need to be sure that their measuring devices—interview questions, survey questions, or methods of observation—are both valid and reliable. Validity refers to the accuracy of the measuring device. In other words, the measuring device must actually measure what it sets out to measure. Reliability refers to the consistency of the measuring device. That is, the measuring device must produce the same results among the same people, or the same results among people who have similar characteristics.

• There are a variety of methods of collecting data for social research about families. Wolf discusses four methods: surveys, experiments, demography, and unstructured observation. There are important advantages and disadvantages to each. Surveys—questionnaires or interviews—are generally used to compare answers to standardized questions about a topic—say, attitudes about abortion—developed by the researcher. Care must be taken in constructing surveys to avoid bias. Experiments are generally used when the researcher wants to explore and directly observe the impact of one variable on other variables. This is done, typically, by comparing a control group, in which the variables remain constant, with experimental groups, in which the variables are manipulated. Demographic data, generally collected by public agencies such as the U.S. Bureau of the Census, is used to track major milestones in the lives of people such as rates of birth, death, marriage, and divorce. Unstructured observation—either as an observer or participant observer—is generally used to explore social and behavioral patterns as they occur naturally, without the interference or manipulation of a researcher.

• Social scientists have developed a number of social theories that help explain how societies operate. Some of these theories are particularly useful for explaining the ways that families operate. The social theories that Wolf applies to the study of the family include structural-functional theory, conflict theory, exchange theory, and systems theory. Wolf discusses the meaning, application, and critique of each of these.

• Structural-functional theory views society as a set of interrelated structures—or parts— with each structure performing a function which is important to the maintenance and stability of society. Society is seen as existing in a state of consensus and equilibrium. This theory can be used to study families in two ways. First, it can be used to examine the family as one of the structures of society and to examine its functions in society. The social functions served by the family include economic production, sexual reproduction, social cohesion, socialization of children, mutual aid, recreation and others. A second way in which structural-functional theory can be used is to look at the structures of the family itself and the functions that they serve.

• Conflict theory assumes that life rarely runs smoothly and conflict is a natural part of social relationships. Rather than explaining society in terms of interrelated structures and functions, conflict theory takes the view that society is based on competition over scarce resources. This competition generally manifests itself in struggles between dominant groups and subordinate groups. It , too, can be applied to the study of families in two ways. First, conflict theory can be used to help explain the part families play in perpetuating the inequality that exists within society. Second, it can be used to explain power relationships within families, such as that between spouses, parents, and children.

• Exchange theory is particularly applicable to the study of the family. Exchange theory sees personal relationships in terms of rewards and costs. The benefits, or rewards, of a relationship are the resources—companionship, sex, affection, services, and so on— which a person receives. Personal relationships, from the viewpoint of exchange theory, are based on a system of exchange of resources among family members. People tend to remain in relationships and/or are satisfied with them when they perceive that their benefits outweigh, or are at least equal to, their costs.

• Systems theory is similar to structural-functional theory in that it views society as a social system made up of interdependent parts. A change in one part of the system has an impact on other parts of the system. An important characteristic of social systems, from the view of systems theory, is that they exist in a state of homeostasis. This means that they have a tendency to maintain a state of stability or equilibrium. Thus, when applied to the family, if one structure is not performing its intended function, another structure may fulfill that function so that the family stability is maintained. For example, if an alcoholic parent fails to fulfill its parental role, a child may begin to act as a parent to the other children, thus enabling the alcoholic parent to continue to fail in its parental role. From this view, families that undergo such systemic changes are perceived as dysfunctional.

KEY TERMS

The following key terms are found in your textbook on the page number indicated in parentheses. In the space provided, write a brief definition of the key term. Then provide an example of the term, such as a culture in which the practice takes place, or people that you might know whose behavior illustrates the term. You could include issues that you might have read about in the news or in a book, or anything else that will illustrate the term and help you remember it. Include any comments from your class discussions or textbook that might help you remember and understand these key terms.

scientific method (p. 33)

variable (p. 33)

dependent variable (p. 33)

independent variable (p. 33)

constant (p. 33)

hypothesis (p. 33)

operationalize a variable (p. 34)

population (p. 34)

sample (p. 35)

representative sample (p. 35)

random sample (p. 35)

response rate (p. 37)

convenience sample (p. 36)

association (p. 38)

causality (p. 38)

control variable (p. 38)

spurious relationship (p. 38)

validity (p. 39)

reliability (p. 39)

survey (p. 40)

respondents (p. 40)

questionnaire (p. 40)

interview (p. 40)

bias (p. 40)

unstructured observation (p. 41)

participant observer (p. 41)

field notes (p. 41)

unstructured interviews (p. 41)

informant (p. 41)

experiment (p. 42)

experimental group (p. 42)

control group (p. 42)

demography (p. 43)

social theories (p. 44)

concepts (p. 44)

structural-functional theory (p. 45)

structures (p. 45)

social institutions (p. 45)

functions (p. 45)

socialization (p. 47)

conflict theory (p. 47)

resources (p. 48)

power (p. 48)

dominant groups (p. 48)

subordinate groups (p. 48)

superstructure of ideology (p. 48)

exchange theory (p. 49)

system of exchange (p. 49)

fictive kin (p. 50)

systems theory (p. 50)

homeostasis (p. 51)

hero (p. 52)

scapegoat (p. 52)

lost child (p. 52)

mascot (p. 52)

NOTES:

PRACTICE TEST

Multiple Choice

1. The scientific method is a way that researchers in which of the following disciplines obtain accurate information about reality:
   a) biology
   b) sociology
   c) psychology
   d) all of the above

2. In the scientific method, something which can change and have more than one value is usually referred to as:
   a) hypothesis
   b) constant
   c) variable
   d) population

3. The behavior or attitude that a study hopes to explain is known as:
   a) the dependent variable
   b) the independent variable
   c) the valid variable
   d) the unknown variable

4. The factor that explains or influences the behavior or attitude that a study hopes to explain is called:
   a) the dependent variable
   b) the independent variable
   c) the valid variable
   d) the unknown variable

5. A prediction about how two or more variables are related is called a:
   a) theory
   b) proposition
   c) hypothesis
   d) conclusion

6. The statement, "Virgins at marriage are less likely to divorce than non-virgins at marriage" is a:
   a) theory
   b) hypothesis
   c) fact
   d) none of the above

7. In the above statement, virginal status is the:
   a) independent variable
   b) dependent variable
   c) descriptive variable
   d) all of the above

8. In the statement found in question 6, divorce is:
   a) independent variable
   b) dependent variable
   c) descriptive variable
   d) all of the above

9. To operationalize a variable means to:
   a) extract the full meaning from it
   b) provide as broad a meaning as possible so that it can be applied easily
   c) find a concrete procedure for measuring it
   d) work on it until you understand what it means

10. In a survey, a researcher asks a series of questions about the types of sexual activity that people engage in and how often. Then, she develops a numerical code which can be applied to each answer in order to calculate a person's level of promiscuity. This process is an example of:
   a) random sampling
   b) reliability
   c) operationalizing a variable
   d) validity

11. The first step in the scientific method is:
   a) selecting a population to study
   b) identifying the independent and dependent variables
   c) developing a hypothesis
   d) formulating a research question

12. The entire group being studied for a particular research project is called the:
   a) population
   b) representative sample
   c) random sample
   d) convenience sample

13. The best way to obtain a representative sample is:
   a) to study the population
   b) to get a random sample of the population
   c) to use a convenience sample
   d) all of the above are equally good representative samples

14. If a correlation exists between an independent and dependent variable, yet the independent variable is not the cause of the dependent variable, this is called:
   a) a spurious relationship
   b) pseudo-causality
   c) pseudo-correlation
   d) non-valid relationship

15. The extent to which a survey or observations measure what the researcher intends them to measure is called:
   a) reliability
   b) validity
   c) operationalization
   d) sampling

16. The extent to which a measuring device, such as a survey, produces consistent results in more than one measurement on the same person is called:
   a) reliability
   b) validity
   c) operationalization
   d) sampling

17. Which of the following is **NOT** a technique used for unstructured observation:
   a) participant observation
   b) unstructured interviews
   c) use of informants
   d) questionnaires

18. An example of a qualitative method would be:
   a) a questionnaire survey in which the researcher counts the number of people who answer a question in a certain way
   b) observing a group in such a way that the researcher can write down descriptions of the behavior and some of the conversations of the group being studied
   c) using census data to calculate the different rates of divorce over a period of time
   d) none of the above are examples of a qualitative method

19. The theory that views society as a set of structures with each structure performing a function which is important to the maintenance and stability of society is called:
a) structural-functional theory
b) conflict theory
c) exchange theory
d) systems theory

20. According to which theory would marital disputes be considered a normal part of family life:
a) structural-functional theory
b) conflict theory
c) exchange theory
d) systems theory

21. Which theory maintains that people tend to remain in relationships when they perceive that the benefits outweigh the costs?
a) structural functional theory
b) conflict theory
c) exchange theory
d) systems theory

22. Which theory views family as a set of interrelated roles that exist in a state of homeostasis?
a) structural functional theory
b) conflict theory
c) exchange theory
d) systems theory

23. In sociological terms, tasks that contribute to the maintenance and continuation of society are:
a) functions
b) institutions
c) resources
d) structures

24. The primary source of socialization of children in American society is:
a) education
b) religion
c) sports
d) family

25. A set of values which supports and justifies the superior power position of the dominant group is known as:
a) a superstructure of ideology
b) homeostasis
c) a system of exchange
d) fictive kin

26. Using exchange theory to examine the family, personal resources include:
a) sex
b) affection
c) child care
d) all of the above

27. Which theory did Carol Stack rely heavily on in her book *All Our Kin,* an analysis of how lower income, mother-headed African American families survive:
a) structural functional theory
b) conflict theory
c) exchange theory
d) systems theory

28. According to Carol Stack, fictive kin are:
a) deceased relatives that play an important part in the daily rituals of African American families
b) heros from novels that African American mothers use as role models for their children
c) close family friends that offer food, shelter, child care and other services to a family in need
d) people who pretend to be friends of single African American mothers, only to defraud them later on

29. Homeostasis refers to:
a) the tendency of a social system, such as a family, to achieve a state of stability and equilibrium
b) a system of exchange between homosexuals
c) the increasing tendency for children to live with their parents until they are married
d) the tendency of a social system to break down

30. From which theory does the concept of dysfunctional families stem?
a) structural functional theory
b) conflict theory
c) exchange theory
d) systems theory

PROJECTS

PROJECT 2. 1 Designing a Research Project to Study the Family

Almost everybody has opinions about issues and problems regarding the family. Sometimes these common sense notions are correct, and sometimes they are not. One of the purposes of social scientific research is to find out accurate information about the family and to help develop theories that can better help us to understand the family. As you read in your textbook, the scientific method is a precise, systematic way to obtain accurate information.

Journal instructions:

1. Think of a social issue, social problem or other topic about the family which you want to find accurate information. If you do not have any ideas, look through the newspapers, news magazines, or the chapter outlines in your text or in this study guide. Find a topic that is interesting to you, but do not be overly ambitious.

2. Review and study the section in the chapter that discusses the steps of the scientific method.

3. Formulate a research question.

4. Specify the dependent variable and one independent variable.

5. Develop a hypothesis.

6. Operationalize the variables, or at least explain how you would operationalize them. Be sure to make sure that your measuring devices are valid and reliable.

7. Select a population to study.

8. Explain how you will select a sample.

9. Describe two techniques you would use to collect your data. Do not simply mention the technique you will use (for example, surveys), but explain exactly some specific things you will do. For example, if you decide to use a survey, develop four or five survey questions.

Option: essay

Using the above information, write an essay (around four to five pages, typed) in which you discuss the research design you developed and your rationale for each step.

Option: bibliography
Use your library's indexes (eg., *Social Science Index, Sociological Abstracts*, and so on) to develop a bibliography of five articles from sociology or other social science journals that deal with the topic for which you designed a research project. Type your bibliography using the format found in the journals or in your textbook.

Option: research paper
Complete the above journal and bibliographic instructions if you have not already done so. Write a paper (around five to seven to nine pages, typed) in which you:

1. Briefly discuss the topic you have chosen to conduct research about and your research design.

2. Compare your research design with the research design (formulation of question, variables, hypotheses, operationalization, and so on) found in two of the articles in the bibliography you developed. Discuss whether or not you feel that the measuring devices used in the articles you selected are reliable and valid.

3. Briefly discuss the conclusions found in each article and discuss how you think your results would compare (similar, different, why?) if your research design were used.

4. Be sure to provide proper documentation throughout the paper and include a reference page.

PROJECT 2. 2 Using Social Theories to Examine Families

Sociologists use a variety of theoretical perspectives to study families. Wolf discusses four of them: structural-functional theory, conflict theory, exchange theory, and systems theory. Review these theories in your text as they are discussed in Chapter 2 before proceeding with the project.

Journal instructions:
1. In your journal, write a summary of what the focus of each of the above theories would be in examining families.

2. For the above theories, develop a list of questions that each theory would lead you to ask about families. For example, for structural functionalism you might ask: What are the major functions provided by families? What structures work to provide these functions? For conflict theory, you might ask: How are conflicts within families the result of power struggles between family members? What are the scarce resources that determine who has the power? And so on. Develop at least four questions for each theory.

3. Examine your own family using the questions you developed for each of the theoretical perspectives. For each of the different theories that you developed questions, spend around two hours observing (if possible) and thinking about relationships within your family. Answer the questions you posed using examples from your own family.

4. Discuss in your journal how these theories might be useful in helping a marriage counselor or someone else who works with families (for example, a clergy-person, divorce mediator, lawyer, and others).

Option: essay
Write an essay (around five pages, typed) in which you discuss your family from the point of view of each of the perspectives from which you observed it and described it in your journal.

Option: bibliography
Use your library's indexes to develop a bibliography of ten to fifteen articles from sociology or other social science journals that discuss themes or issues you addressed in your journal. Try to find articles that use the theories that you discussed. Type your bibliography using the bibliographic style found in the sociology journal or in your textbook,

Option: research paper
If you have not done so already, complete the above journal, essay and bibliography instructions. Write a paper, around seven to ten pages, in which you discuss your family using a sociological perspective. Integrate your observations of your family with sociological ideas found within at least five articles from your bibliography. Do the following:

1. Use ideas and information from five of the articles in your bibliography to explain some of the issues about your family that you discussed in the journal assignment for this project.

2. Use information collected in your journal assignment above to illustrate and discuss some of the ideas found in some of the articles in your bibliography.

3. Provide proper documentation of your references throughout the paper and include a reference page.

CHAPTER 3

GENDER

CHAPTER OUTLINE

Traditional Gender Roles
- Traditional Male Role
- Strain in the Traditional Male Role
- Traditional Female Role
- Strain in the Traditional Female Role

Acquiring Gender Roles
- Social Learning Theory
- Cognitive Developmental Theory
- Identification Theory

Changing Gender Roles in Society
- Work and Gender
- Implications for Divorce and Widowhood
- Gender Roles in Two-Earner Marriage
- African American Families

Gender Inequality
- Structural-Functional Theory
- Women as Part of Nature Argument
- Conflict Theory
- Feminist Theory

CHAPTER LEARNING OBJECTIVES

After studying this chapter, you should be able to:

- discuss traditional gender role expectations for males and females and the strains inherent in each;
- discuss how people acquire gender roles through social learning theory, cognitive development theory, and identification theory;
- discuss how and why gender roles have changed over the course of American history;
- discuss the implications of changing gender roles for the workplace, for divorce or widowhood, and for two-earner families;
- discuss the differences between African-American two-earner marriages and white two-earner marriages;
- provide explanations of gender inequality from the perspectives of structural-functional theory, woman as part of nature argument, conflict theory, and feminist theory, and to offer critiques of these theories.

KEY POINTS FOR REVIEW

- Traditional gender roles for males and females are stereotyped as instrumental and expressive, respectively. Typically, the male instrumental role emphasizes rationality, aggression, goal-orientation, and competitiveness. The female expressive role stresses nurturance, peace-making, and emotional expression. Gender roles have an strong impact on the way we see ourselves and on the ways in which we live our lives.

- There are significant strains for males and females stemming from their respective instrumental and expressive role expectations. The expectations that the male be the provider and protector are difficult to fulfill, especially in today's economy. Additionally, men who desire to be nurturing may have a difficult time expressing themselves because of the expectations associated with an instrumental role. The expectations for women to be care-givers may lead them to lose touch with their own needs and may lead to identity problems. Further, women who work outside the home are faced with the additional expectations associated with being a homemaker and mother.

- People are not born with gender roles; they acquire them. There are a variety of theories that explain how we acquire our gender roles. Three of them include social learning theory, cognitive development theory, and identification theory. Social learning theory holds that children acquire gender roles by observing and imitating their parents and through parental reinforcement of gender behavior. A criticism of this theory is that it sees children as passive learners who play no part in acquiring gender roles. By contrast, cognitive development theory contends that children form mental categories of appropriate gender behavior and then actively seek out information about what is considered appropriate for their gender. Identification theory maintains that both male and female children identify with the mother since she is typically the primary caregiver. As a result, females develop a strong gender identity, yet have a difficult time developing a distinct sense of separation from others. Conversely, males have a more difficult time developing a strong gender identity, but have a stronger sense of separation, stronger ego boundaries.

• Gender roles have not remained constant over time, but have changed over the course of American history. In fact, the division between the instrumental male role and the expressive female role did not develop until the nineteenth century. This occurred largely with the advent of industrialization around 1830. With the separation of the workplace from the home, male and female roles became more specialized. However, we are beginning to see a shift back toward greater androgyny and gender equality. Yet, important issues regarding gender inequality persist. In employment, there is still a significant amount of gender segregation of men and women into separate jobs, and gender stratification continues to yield more higher paying positions for men than for women. This has an especially negative impact on women who experience divorce and widowhood and contributes to the feminization of poverty. Even with the shift toward more two-earner families and more androgynous gender roles, women continue to do two thirds of the housework.

• African American marriages tend to be more egalitarian than white marriages largely because of the limited occupational opportunities, low wages, and frequent unemployment faced by African American men. This has led them to play a more important role in child care and taking care of the home.

• There are a number of theories that explain the persistence of gender inequality in the family and in the workplace. Wolf examines structural-functional theory, the women-as-part-of-nature argument, conflict theory, and feminist theory. Structural-functional theory argues that the necessity for two specialized roles within the family, an instrumental role and an expressive role, naturally leads to the development of these roles for males and females respectively. An important criticism lies in its assumption that male dominance is natural and that the instrumental role must be concentrated into a single social role.

• The women-as-part-of-nature argument maintains that male dominance and female subordination is universal because of the fact of women's biological reproductive functions. The theory states that males find it natural to subordinate women because the reproductive functions of women cause them to be associated with "animal-like nature" and male activities of hunting, clearing land and growing crops represents mastery over and taming of nature. A significant criticism of this theory is that male dominance is not found in all societies. Further, the reproductive functions of women are interpreted differently in different cultures, some of which view women as more powerful than men.

• According to conflict theory, the basis for male dominance over women in the family lies in the male's control over economic resources in the larger society. Conflict theory maintains that male dominance arose as a way of making sure that children of the wife were produced by the husband and were thus rightful heirs to his property. Other resources that lead to male dominance include educational attainment and occupational status. According to conflict theory, the partner with the most resources holds the most power. An important criticism of this theory is that it overlooks other personal resources, such as sex, love, and companionship, which can also provide a partner with influence in a relationship. Further, conflict theory overlooks the important part that gender role socialization plays in upholding stereotypical gender roles.

• Feminist theory, which derives from conflict theory, contains five basic elements: 1) Gender is a fundamental aspect in all social relationships. 2) The everyday experiences of women are important. 3) The subordination of women in society and in the family may be manifested in wife battering, an unequal division of household labor, and the sexual abuse of female children. 4) Social change designed to bring about equality between males and females is necessary. 4) Social images and cultural beliefs which exaggerate male-female differences that are used to legitimize the subordination of women must be examined. A criticism of this theory is that it puts too much emphasis on the inequalities faced by women and not enough emphasis on the gratification that male-female relationships provide.

NOTES:

KEY TERMS

The following key terms are found in your textbook on the page number indicated in parentheses. In the space provided, write a brief definition of the key term. Then provide an example of the term, such as a culture in which the practice takes place, or people that you might know whose behavior illustrates the term. You could include issues that you might have read about in the news or in a book, or anything else that will illustrate the term and help you remember it. Include any comments from your class discussions or textbook that might help you remember and understand these key terms.

gender role (p. 60)

gender (p. 60)

sex (p. 60)

instrumental role (p. 61)

expressive role (p. 61)

bipolar roles (p. 61)

social learning theory (p. 64)

positive reinforcement (p. 64)

cognitive development (p. 66)

gender constancy (p. 66)

role model (p. 66)

schema (p. 66)

gender schema (p. 66)

identification theory (p. 68)

identification (p. 68)

issue of separation (p. 68)

androgyny (p. 70)

gender segregation (p. 71)

gender stratification (p. 71)

sexual harassment (p. 72)

feminization of poverty (p. 72)

second shift (p. 73)

bi-national families (p. 74)

structural functional theory of gender inequality (p. 75)

women-as-part-of-nature argument (p. 76)

overgeneralize (p. 78)

matrilineal (p. 77)

matrilocal residence(p. 77)

conflict theory of inequality (p. 79)

resources (p. 79)

power (p. 79)

feminist theory of inequality (p. 80)

PRACTICE TEST

Multiple Choice

1. A set of social expectations associated with being male or female is referred to as:
   a) gender
   b) sex
   c) gender role
   d) sex role

2. Traditional stereotypes of gender roles are:
   a) male instrumental and female expressive roles
   b) male expressive and female instrumental roles
   c) males and females are expected to follow instrumental roles
   d) males and females have both instrumental and expressive roles

3. One problem with social expectations associated with traditional gender roles is that they ignore:
   a) the fact that women are naturally better leaders than men
   b) the similarities between men and women as well as the differences within each gender
   c) the fact that men are naturally better at nurturing children than women
   d) none of the above

4. The source of a husband's identity has traditionally come from:
   a) his role as father in the family
   b) his role as husband
   c) his work around the house
   d) his employment outside the home

5. Studies show that fathers who are active in child care or home management:
   a) report considerable role conflict and stress in attempting to combine work and family responsibilities
   b) report higher levels of satisfaction in their employment and a greater sense of peace within their lives
   c) report less satisfaction in their employment
   d) report enhanced sex lives with their wives

6. African American men have traditionally been actively involved in child care primarily because:
   a) they have better nurturing qualities than white American men
   b) African American women tend to be more dominant than white American women
   c) African American women have historically had higher employment rates than African American men
   d) African American children need more aggressive socialization on the part of parents

7. One of the negative effects of traditional male and female gender roles can be found in the sexual relationships of distressed couples. A study of married couples found that in unhappy marriages:
   a) husbands tended to be less satisfied with their marital sex than their wives
   b) wives tended to be less satisfied with their marital sex than their husbands
   c) both husbands and wives were equally dissatisfied with their marital sex
   d) the sex life of married couples has little to do with traditional gender roles

8. Among some Native American cultures, the "berdache" are:
   a) women who adopt a traditional male role for the purpose of gaining power
   b) men who adopt a traditional female role because they are not comfortable with the traditional male role
   c) transvestites who are stigmatized in order to serve as an example that traditional gender roles are sacred and cannot be changed
   d) children of homosexual marriages

9. One way in which gender affects the patterns of communication which occurs in family is that:
   a) children of both sexes reveal more information about themselves to their mothers than to their fathers
   b) mothers tend to hear information concerning a broad range of topics, whereas fathers tend to hear mainly about task oriented topics from children
   c) fathers tend to hear information concerning a broad range of topics, whereas mothers tend to hear only about emotional issues
   d) a and b above

10. The acquisition of gender roles begins to occur:
   a) at birth
   b) when children begin to play games
   c) upon entrance into elementary school
   d) during adolescence

11. Observation, imitation, and reinforcement are key elements in which of the following theories of gender role socialization?
a) cognitive development theory
b) identification theory
c) social learning theory
d) structural-functional theory

12. Which theory of gender role socialization views children as active processors of information regarding their own gender?
a) cognitive development theory
b) identification theory
c) social learning theory
d) structural-functional theory

13. One important criticism of the social learning theory of gender role socialization is that:
a) it has been proven that males and females learn differently
b) gender roles are not learned, rather they are inherently part of our biological make-up
c) it assumes that the child is a passive learner
d) it assumes that children play an active role in their own socialization

14. Identification theory argues that as a result of both male and female children identifying with the mother:
a) the male child has a problem developing a separate sense of himself
b) the female child has a problem developing a separate sense of herself
c) the male develops a strong sense of gender identity
d) the female has a problem developing a strong sense of gender identity

15. The stereotypical male-instrumental and female-expressive roles:
a) have always existed in American society
b) are biologically universal and have only recently begun to change
c) developed with the advent of industrialization and the separation of the workplace from home
d) became entrenched in most cultures during the hunting and gathering phase of existence

16. As gender roles for males and females have become more androgynous:
a) husbands and wives tend to share housework equally
b) gender segregation in the workplace has disappeared
c) gender stratification in the workplace has virtually been eliminated
d) both gender segregation and gender stratification in the workplace still exist

17. No-fault divorce laws which have been adopted by almost all states have led to:
a) an increase in the feminization of poverty
b) insure that after a divorce, both spouses and the children will be equally well off
c) benefiting women and children at the expense of the husband
d) insure that above all else, the children's standard of living will not decrease

18. The theory of gender inequality that says that male dominance in the family is natural because it meets the needs of the family is:
a) structural-functional theory
b) feminist theory
c) the women-as-part-of-nature-argument
d) conflict theory

19. The conflict theory of gender inequality argues that:
a) male dominance in the family is natural and is at the root of conflict between husbands and wives
b) male dominance in the family is the result of males having more resources in society in general
c) husband and wives will always be in a state of conflict as a result of biological inequities that exist between males and females
d) the conflict that exists between husbands and wives because of inequality is healthy to a relationship

20. Which theory of gender inequality argues that gender equality must actively be pursued because relationships between women and men are a fundamental aspect of social life?
a) women-as-part-of-nature-argument
b) structural functional theory
c) feminist theory
d) conflict theory

NOTES:

PROJECTS

PROJECT 3. 1 Acquiring Gender Roles

Gender roles are expectations associated with being male and female. We are not born with our gender roles. **Gender role socialization** is the name of the process that explains how we acquire our gender roles. There are a number of theories of gender role socialization. Three of them include **social learning theory, cognitive development theory, and identification theory**. The objective of this project is to have you observe how people acquire gender roles and to use your observations to help you better understand these three theories.

Journal instructions:

1. Before beginning this project, re-read the section in Chapter 3 on acquiring gender roles. For each theory, make a list of situations and examples in which gender role socialization might occur both for yourself and for children.

2. For an entire week, keep a journal in which your record as thoroughly as possible every instance of gender role socialization that you experience and that you observe other people experiencing. These include observations of interpersonal relationships (yours and others around you), family, friends, advertisements, school, media (television, radio, newspapers, magazines), and so on. Briefly describe each situation and event and discuss the underlying gender role message being sent. Pay particular attention to situations which involve gender role socialization among children.

3. At the end of the week, do a content analysis of your observations. That is, organize the types of socialization experiences that you recorded into categories (for example, everyday interaction, education, religion, family, and so on).

4. Next, organize your observations in terms of how they might illustrate each of the gender role theories you read about in the chapter. That is, which examples could be used to illustrate social learning theory? Which could be used to illustrate cognitive development theory? Which could be used to illustrate identification theory? You may use your examples more than one time.

Option: essay

Using the above information, write an essay (around four to five pages, typed) in which you use the theories of gender role socialization to discuss the observations you made in your journal throughout the week.

Option: bibliography
Use your library's indexes (eg., *Social Science Index, Sociological Abstracts*, and so on) to develop a bibliography of ten articles from sociology or other social science journals that deal with gender role socialization. Type your bibliography using the format found in the journals or in your textbook.

Option: research paper
Complete the above journal and bibliographic instructions if you have not already done so. Write a paper (around seven to nine pages, typed) in which you:

1. Briefly discuss the process of how we acquire gender roles and review some theories of gender role socialization.

2. Discuss the way in which you collected the data for the journal observations.

3. Use information from five of the journal articles from the bibliography you developed and theories of gender role socialization to discuss the information you collected through your journal observations.

4. Be sure to provide proper documentation throughout the paper and include a reference page.

PROJECT 3. 2 Gender Inequality in the Workplace

Even though people are developing more **androgynous gender roles**—that is, roles that exhibit both masculine and feminine traits—gender inequality in the workplace still exists. It exists primarily in the form of **gender segregation** and **gender stratification.** Men and women tend to be employed to do different types of work and for unequal pay. There tends to be a **split labor market** for men and women. The **primary labor market** employs people who are on a career path that will likely advance them to higher-level positions. The **secondary labor market** contains jobs that contain little, if any, chance of professional advancement. The purpose of this project is to have you examine the extent to which gender segregation and stratification exist in the workplace and to consider why.

Journal instructions:
1. Identify a large corporation or other organization that employs many people, such as the college you attend, an insurance company, a hospital, or any large business for which you can obtain access of a list of types of employment and the names of the employees. The easiest choice for you will be the college that you attend.

2. Obtain a list of all of the types of employment that exist at the place of employment you selected (for example, secretaries, administrators, faculty members, groundkeepers, cafeteria workers, and so on). This can be obtained from the director of human resources or other public records, such as the college catalogue. Once you obtain the list of types of employment, do the following:

a) Read through the list of personnel and keep a list of each different type of employment or position at the organization you selected. If you selected your college, this probably will appear in the back of the college catalogue.

b) Count the number of men and the number of women in each employment position. Then, calculate the percentage of women and men that do each particular job. (For example, ninety five percent of the secretaries are female, five percent are men, and so on).

c) Find out the number of members there are on the Board of Directors and what percentage are men and women.

3. After you have completed the above, interview someone who works in each of the positions you identified. Briefly describe, in your journal, what they do, the level of difficulty of their job, and the likelihood for professional advancement.

4. Rank the jobs in terms of what you think the salaries are, from the highest to the lowest. You do not have to know the actual salaries.

5. Based on all of the above data that you collected, divide the jobs into two lists: primary market and secondary market. What percentage of the employees in each market are female and what percentage are male?

6. Interview two women and two men who work at the place of employment you identified. Be sure to assure them that their answers are strictly confidential and be sure to honor that commitment. Try to interview two people from the primary labor market and two from the secondary labor market. In your journal, write down their answers to the following questions:

a) Do men and women in the primary labor market (mention the jobs you have in your primary market list) have the same chances for professional advancement?

b) Are there any male traditions, stereotypes, or prejudices of women that still exist at this place of employment—either overtly or covertly—that impede the advancement of women there? If so, what are they?

c) Are there any ways in which women are denied the same opportunities for advancement as men—again, either overtly or covertly?

Option: essay
Using the information that you collected in your journal above, write an essay in which you discuss the extent to which gender segregation and gender stratification exists at the place of employment you studied. Do they exist? To what extent? Why? If you find that gender segregation and stratification exist, use the theories of gender inequality discussed in Chapter 3 of your textbook to offer some possible explanations. Did you find any evidence in your observations or interviews that support any of the theories? If so, discuss.

Option: bibliography
Use your library's indexes to develop a bibliography of ten to fifteen articles from sociology or other social science journals that discuss gender segregation, gender stratification, primary and secondary labor markets, and gender inequality in the workplace. Type your bibliography using the bibliographic style found in the sociology journal or in your textbook.

Option: research paper
If you have not done so already, complete the above journal, essay and bibliography instructions. Write a paper, around seven to ten pages, in which you discuss gender inequality in the workplace, using the research you conducted as a case study. Integrate your research with sociological ideas found within at least five articles from your bibliography. Do the following:

1. Use ideas and information from around five of the articles in your bibliography to explain how different labor markets (primary and secondary) affect men and women differently.

2. Use information collected in your journal assignment to illustrate and discuss some of the ideas found in some of the articles in your bibliography.

3. Provide proper documentation of your references throughout the paper and include a reference page.

NOTES:

CHAPTER 4

FALLING IN LOVE: SEXUALITY AND DATING

CHAPTER OUTLINE

Sexual Attitudes and Behavior
- The Sexual Revolution
- Sexual Attitudes and Behavior Today
- The Double Standard
- The Selfish Standard
- Oral-Genital Sex

Sexual Communication in Dating
- Interpreting Behavior
- Token Resistance
- Unwanted Sex

Traditional Gender Roles
- Traditional Female Gender Role
- Traditional Male Gender Role

Dating and Sexuality After Divorce
- Is the Sexually Liberated Divorced Person a Myth?
- Divorce, Dating and Stress
- Courtship Prior to Remarriage

From Romantic Love to Companionate Love
- Characteristics of Romantic Love
- Does Romance Have a Biological Basis?
- Characteristics of Companionate Love

Sternberg's Triangular Theory of Love

Reiss's Wheel Theory of Love

Love Relationships and Social Networks
- Withdrawal-Integration Hypothesis
- Romeo and Juliet Hypothesis
- Approval of Social Networks

Love Ideology
- Defining Love by Its Feminine Expression
- Traditional Love Ideology: Love as Self-Sacrifice
- Modern Love Ideology: Love as Self-Development

Love and Relationship Satisfaction
- Exchange Theory
- Mark's Theory of the Three-Cornered Self

CHAPTER LEARNING OBJECTIVES

After studying this chapter, you should be able to:

- discuss how and why sexual attitudes and behaviors have changed over the past few decades;
- identify and discuss specific problems related to sexual communication in dating;
- discuss male and female views about initiating sexual relationships and the impact of traditional gender roles on their respective views;
- discuss sexual and dating patterns, and the interrelationship between them, of divorced people;
- identify and discuss six styles of loving and the loving styles associated with males and females;
- identify and discuss the components of Sternberg's triangular theory of love and the different ways they can combine to form different types of love relationships;
- identify and discuss the stages of Reiss's Wheel Theory of Love and their relationship to each other;
- discuss the effects of love relationships on social networks and the effects of social networks on love relationships;
- discuss the impact of a traditional love ideology and a modern love ideology on love relationships;
- discuss how exchange theory and Mark's Theory of the Three-Cornered Self explain how relationship satisfaction affects love.

KEY POINTS FOR REVIEW

• A societal emphasis on sexual experimentation, the introduction of the birth control pill, the legalization of abortion, and delaying of marriage has increased the opportunities for sexual activity over the past few decades. In particular, more unmarried Americans are having sexual intercourse within less committed relationships than was the case in the 1950s. In 1953, Kinsey reported that only 23% of women had experienced intercourse by age 20. By 1970, women were twice as likely to have experienced premarital intercourse than in 1953.

• Although the double standard of the 1950s which allowed male promiscuity and required female virginity has faded somewhat, some aspects of the double standard still exist. Men are still expected to initiate sex and women are expected to appear less interested. Women, but not men, are still expected to limit their number of sexual partners. Further, it is still considered more acceptable for men than for women to engage in casual sex.

• Researchers have reported that a selfish standard exists when it comes to picking a marriage partner for themselves. This means that many people who allow themselves to be sexually active prefer marriage partners who are without previous experience in either intercourse or oral-genital sex.

• Sexual communication is an important issue in dating, and people often have difficulty both in interpreting their partner's behavior and desires and appropriately expressing their own. Males often perceive that if a woman wears revealing clothing, asks a man out on a date, or hints that she is available for a date that she is necessarily interested in having sex. Behavior which male viewers saw as exhibiting sexual interest are more perceived by females as, simply, friendly behavior. Another problem of interpretation stems from a traditional sexual script that encourages women to behave in a resistant manner when the man makes sexual overtures. As a result, men are sometimes confused as to whether a women is offering "token resistance" or her resistance is honest. The traditional sexual script has also led both men and women to participate in unwanted sex.

• Traditional gender roles affect the way in which men and women view the initiation of a sexual relationship differently. The woman traditionally has been expected to play the role of the "gatekeeper" and to set limits in sexual situations. Yet, the traditional female role that encourages passivity, nurturance, helpfulness, and submissiveness often inhibit the woman from dealing effectively with unwanted sexual advances. At the same time, the traditional male role encourages men to have a favorable view of casual sex, to be perpetually interested in sex, to be dominant and sexually assertive, and to initiate sexual advances. The contrast between these two sets of social expectations often promotes adversarial sexual encounters.

• A recent study of the sexual sexual behavior of divorced people has found that they are much more sexually conservative than a classic study conducted in the 1970s depicted them to be. This discrepancy may be due to a flawed sample used in the earlier study, or it might be that sexual behavior has actually become more conservative over the past two decades. Nevertheless, the difficulty of navigating the dating world and dealing with sexual issues adds to the stress of being divorced. Much of the stress of divorce and dating is reduced when a person finds a compatible partner and enters cohabitation. One study showed that courtship patterns of divorced mothers typically progressed from dating to partial cohabitation to full-time cohabitation.

• Social scientists have identified six types of love: eros (passionate and emotionally intense), mania (emotionally intense, insecure, jealous and possessive), agape (selfless and altruistic), pragma (practical), storge (companionate and friendly), and ludus (playful and flirtatious). Men and women tend to have different love styles. Women tend more toward storge, mania, pragma and agape love. Men tend more toward eros and ludus.

• Sexual behavior often takes place within the context of romantic love. Romantic love—an intense, erotic attraction and yearning which idealizes the partner—is characterized by intrusive thoughts, mood swings, idealization, exclusivity and fear of rejection. Some biologically oriented psychologists and anthropologists have suggested that the experience of romance is related to a biochemical response in the brain, but not all agree with this. Some researchers have found that over time, romantic love gives way to companionate love—a strong and enduring affection which is more peaceful and comfortable than romantic love.

• Robert Sternberg, in his triangular theory of love, has argued that it is possible to maintain love relationships that are romantic as well as companionate. Sternberg maintains that love has three components—passion, intimacy and commitment. While these three components often exist in varying degrees in a love relationship, Sternberg argues that each must be present for love to be complete.

• Ira Reiss's wheel theory of love maintains that a person goes through four stages when falling in love—rapport to self-revelation to mutual dependency to intimacy need fulfillment. This theory says that a relationship can move in the direction of greater or lesser love. For partners who are becoming less engaged with each other, the direction is from intimacy need fulfillment to rapport.

• Love relationships are both affected by and affect the social networks of the lovers. The withdrawal-integration hypothesis says that as people fall in love, they tend to withdraw from their social network of friends. Then, as they begin to detach from the love relationship, people become reintegrated with friends. The Romeo and Juliet hypothesis states that in quickly developing love relationships, when parents express opposition to a romance, the romance grows stronger. However, this is not the case for more slowly developing relationships. In most cases, though, the approval of the social network tends to strengthen the love relationship.

• We tend to judge our experiences with romantic love by comparing them to a love ideology—a set of beliefs or cultural ideals related to love. Love ideology throughout the twentieth century has been based on traditional feminine-expressive and male-instrumental gender role stereotypes. The love ideology in American culture places greater value on the female style of demonstrating love—that is, through verbal expressions of love and emotional closeness—and thus, women are expected to be more skilled than men at love relationships. This can place stress on women by assigning them the primary responsibility for making the love relationship work. This underlies a traditional love ideology that defines love as self-sacrifice, especially on the part of the woman. The traditional love ideology has begun to shift to a modern love ideology that defines love as self-development. This ideology sees love as a means to self-development and fulfillment for both partners and, again, has particular significance for women.

• There are a number of theories that try to explain what leads to satisfaction in love relationships. Exchange theory maintains that people tend to be satisfied with a love relationship when they perceive that the rewards which they receive are equal to the rewards which they provide to the partner. Mark's Theory of the Three-Cornered Self states that relationship satisfaction is based upon the fulfillment of three identities within the individuals: a person's identity as part of the couple, a person's social identity that is derived from things such as a job, hobbies, and friends other than the partner, and a person's personal identity based on one's feelings, past history, inner experience and thoughts. Satisfaction with the relationship is highest when both partners give equal attention to each of these identities.

NOTES:

KEY TERMS

The following key terms are found in your textbook on the page number indicated in parentheses. In the space provided, write a brief definition of the key term. Then provide an example of the term, such as a culture in which the practice takes place, or people that you might know whose behavior illustrates the term. You could include issues that you might have read about in the news or in a book, or anything else that will illustrate the term and help you remember it. Include any comments from your class discussions or textbook that might help you remember and understand these key terms.

the sexual revolution (p. 87)

double standard (p. 89)

selfish standard (p. 89)

sexual scripts (p. 93)

token resistance (p. 93)

date rape (p. 92)

traditional female gender role for sexual relationships (p. 95)

traditional male gender role for sexual relationships (p. 95)

romantic love (p. 98)

companionate love (p. 98)

eros (p. 100)

mania (p. 100)

agape (p. 100)

pragma (p. 100)

storge (p. 100)

ludus (p. 100)

two-component theory of emotions (p. 101)

PEA (phenylethylamine) (p. 102)

Sternberg's triangular theory of love (p. 102)

passion (p. 103)

commitment (p. 103)

intimacy (p. 103)

Reiss's wheel theory of love (p. 103)

rapport (p. 103)

self-revelation (p. 104)

mutual dependency (p. 104)

intimacy need fulfillment (p. 104)

social networks (p. 105)

withdrawal-integration hypothesis (p. 105)

Romeo and Juliet hypothesis (p. 105)

love ideology (p. 106)

expressive demonstration of love (p. 107)

instrumental demonstration of love (p. 107)

love as self-sacrifice (p. 107)

love as self-development (p. 108)

vital marriage (p. 107)

exchange theory of satisfaction with love relationships (p. 109)

Mark's theory of the three-cornered self (p. 110)

autonomy (p. 111)

PRACTICE TEST

Multiple Choice

1. With regard to sexual situations and dating, the sexual revolution:
    a) has clarified expectations for both males and females
    b) has confused expectations for both males and females
    c) has clarified expectations for males but not for females
    d) has clarified expectations for females but not for males

2. Sexual attitudes and behavior have changed dramatically over the last half century. For example, in the 1970s:
    a) women were twice as likely to have experienced premarital intercourse than during the 1950s
    b) women were half as likely to have experienced premarital intercourse than during the 1950s
    c) men were less likely to have experienced premarital intercourse than during the 1950s
    d) most men and women were likely to have sexual intercourse within the first three dates

3. Changes in sexual attitudes and behavior over the past three decades are largely the result of:
    a) the introduction of the birth control pill
    b) the legalization of abortion
    c) an extended dating period due to more women entering higher education and the labor force
    d) all of the above

4. Today, the average age at first intercourse for women is:
    a) between 13 and 16
    b) between 16 and 17
    c) between 17 and 19
    d) between 19 and 23

5. The double standard which allowed male sexual promiscuity while requiring female virginity:
    a) has all but disappeared
    b) has given way to a new double standard which encourages females to initiate sex, but discourages males from doing so
    c) has faded, but many aspects still remain
    d) has not changed at all, despite the sexual revolution

6. The "selfish standard" regarding preference for marriage partners indicates that:
   a) males prefer women who are experienced sexually so that they can have increased satisfaction early in the marriage
   b) females prefer men who are experienced sexually so that they can have increased satisfaction early in the marriage
   c) both males and females prefer experienced sexual partners
   d) both males and females prefer partners who are without previous sexual experience

7. According to research about sexual behavior among high school and college students, which of the following is <u>NOT</u> a reason that dating partners sometimes use oral-genital sex as a substitute for intercourse:
   a) a desire to retain one's virginity
   b) having a high level of religious belief
   c) a desire to gain more sexual experience
   d) a desire to postpone intercourse until marriage

8. Males often perceive that a female that they date is interested in sex if:
   a) she wears short skirts or low-cut clothing
   b) she asks a man out on a date
   c) she hints that she is available for a date
   d) females display any of the above behaviors

9. "Sexual scripts" are:
   a) ways in which males and females act in pornographic films and sex manuals
   b) the sexual roles that males and females are encouraged to adopt in a society
   c) the language that people use during sexual activity
   d) the language that people use to indicate that they are sexually interested in each other

10. In dating situations, sexual scripts can lead to:
    a) problems with interpreting how each other feels with regard to sex
    b) token resistance
    c) unwanted sex
    d) all of the above

11. The fact that token resistance is part of the sexual script for women suggests that:
    a) women never know if they really want to have sex or not
    b) women never express their true feelings about whether or not they want to have sex
    c) most female resistance to sex is dishonest
    d) women are still stigmatized if they express an interest in sex

12. Submitting to unwanted sexual activity:
a) occurs much more often for women than for men
b) occurs for men as well as for women
c) rarely occurs since there has been more attention called to sexually transmitted diseases
d) none of the above

13. Sometimes women have difficulty dealing effectively with unwanted sexual advances because:
a) the traditional female gender role often leads women to defer to the man's decisions and place the needs of the man above hers
b) traditional female gender roles have inhibited women from realizing their innate sexual nature for so long that they seize the opportunity to have sex whenever possible
c) when it comes to matters of sex, it is difficult to control one's desires
d) an extremely skilled male love makes it difficult for a woman to say no

14. Sometimes men have difficult dealing effectively with unwanted sexual advances because:
a) the American image of masculinity depicts the man as being perpetually interested in sex
b) men sometimes fear that their female partners with think that they are homosexual if they refuse a sexual advance
c) men are encouraged to gain sexual experience whenever possible
d) all of the above

15. Recent research on divorced people revealed that:
a) divorced people are much more sexually liberal than they were two decades ago
b) there has not been much change in divorced people's sexual behavior over the past few decades
c) divorced people are more sexually conservative than they were two decades ago
d) divorced people are not likely to have much sex until they remarry

16. Divorced persons who cohabitate with a compatible partner:
a) are less satisfied with their sex lives than divorced persons who have many dating partners
b) experience more tension than before they cohabitate because of heightened fear of a failed relationship
c) tend to enjoy greater happiness and better physical health than other divorced people
d) experience greater economic hardship than before they cohabitated

17. Social scientists generally believe that love relationships:
a) tend to be characterized more by romantic love than by companionate love
b) have elements of romantic and companionate love at various times in the relationship
c) tend to be characterized more by companionate love than romantic love
d) tend to remain in the style—either romantic or companionate—in which they first began

18. Which of the following types of love are more likely to be characteristic male love styles?
a) eros and ludus
b) agape and storge
c) mania and pragma
d) agape and pragma

19. Which of the following is <u>NOT</u> true of people whose love relationship has moved from romantic love to companionate love?
a) they report that the lack of passion in their lives leads to barriers in communication with each other
b) they report that they are not as burdened with intrusive thoughts and can concentrate on productive work better
c) they report less of a need for exclusivity in friendships and relationships with others
d) they report fewer mood swings between ecstasy and despair

20. Sternberg's Triangular Theory of Love says that the following three components must be present for real love:
a) physiological arousal, emotional arousal, commitment
b) rapport, self-revelation, mutual dependency
c) passion, intimacy, commitment
d) passion, intimacy, mutual dependency

21. Sternberg feels that the component of love that is least under conscious control and is most difficult to maintain over time is:
a) physiological arousal
b) commitment
c) rapport
d) passion

22. Reiss's Wheel Theory of Love states that:
a) the love relationship is stable and all people progress through it similarly
b) a relationship can move in the direction of greater or lesser love
c) love relationships invariably move in the direction of greater love
d) love relationships usually start out very intense at the beginning and then experience a natural rotation to a relationship in which the partners are less engaged with one another

23. The kind of relationship that people falling in love have with their social network of friends and relatives:
a) is usually unaffected by their love relationship
b) tends to change when people fall in love
c) is usually a slow, steady, and continuous process of detachment
d) always improves

24. Love ideology throughout the twentieth century has assigned women the primary responsibility for maintaining love relationships because:
   a) it is believed that women understand love better than men and are better at expressing love
   b) women have a natural, biological drive to become mothers
   c) men are too interested in sex to be interested in maintaining a love relationship
   d) it is believed that women have a hormone that enables them to be more committed to a relationship

25. The traditional love ideology that expected women to put their needs aside and concentrate on filling the needs of their partner is called the ideology of:
   a) love as self-fulfillment
   b) love as self-development
   c) love as self-sacrifice
   d) love as self-integration

26. The modern love ideology urges women to:
   a) seek their own personal fulfillment in education and a career rather than focus solely on their husbands
   b) continue to focus primarily on their husbands and families, but also to seek their own personal fulfillment
   c) postpone marriage as long as possible
   d) enter into marriage early so that their husbands can provide them with emotional and financial support

27. Exchange theory maintains that when it comes to love relationships:
   a) weighing the rewards and costs of a relationship is not relevant
   b) people are more satisfied with a relationship if they believe that they are contributing more to it than their partner
   c) American sexual scripts have socialized people into wanting variety in their love relationships which leads to a tendency to want to change lovers
   d) people tend to be more satisfied with a love relationship when they perceive that the rewards they receive are equal to the rewards they provide to their partner

28. One recent test of exchange theory found that:
   a) when women feel that they are contributing more to the relationship than their partner, they would ask their partners to increase their contribution to the relationship
   b) when women feel that they are contributing less to the relationship than their partner, they would try to increase their contribution
   c) when men feel that there is an imbalance in the relationship, they are likely to do nothing
   d) all of the above

29. According to Mark's theory of the three-cornered self, individuals are more satisfied with a relationship when:
a) their identity as being part of a couple becomes more important than their personal identity
b) their identity as individuals becomes more important than their identity as being part of a couple
c) their identity as being part of a couple and their individual identities all receive attention
d) the partners are neither concerned with their identity as a couple nor their individual identities

30. In love relationships, the person who backs away emotionally:
a) tends to have less power in the relationship than the other partner
b) tends to have more power in the relationship than the other partner
c) tends to be more dependent on the other partner for other rewards, such as physical, emotional, and psychological
d) tends to want to restore balance to the relationship

NOTES:

PROJECTS

PROJECT 4. 1 Are There Gender and Age Differences in Sexual Communication in

Both men and women have difficulty communicating to their dating partners what sexual activities are appropriate and inappropriate. Difficulties in **interpreting the behavior** or desires of the other partner, **token resistance** on the part of women, and **unwanted sex** (including **date rape)** for both men and women often stem from a lack of clarity in communication about sex. Is this true of people all ages? Are the problems different for males and for females? This project is intended to have you explore issues related to sexual communication in dating. It will also give you some experience in collecting qualitative data through interviews.

Journal instructions:

1. Before beginning this project, re-read the section in Chapter 4 on sexual communication in dating. In your journal, list and explain the issues related to sexual communication in dating that your book discusses, and add others that you might be able to think of.

2. For each of the issues that you listed above, develop examples of three scenarios in which the problem might occur. For example, for **difficulties in interpreting behavior** you might describe a specific situation in which a male takes a woman home after a date and she invites him in for a while before he goes home. In a gesture of courtesy and cordiality, she offers him a cup of coffee, puts on some music, and offers to show him some photographs of a recent trip she took. Fill in as much detail as you want, but try to keep your descriptions to within three or four sentences each. Don't forget to create three scenarios for each of the issues in sexual communication that you listed. Use your textbook for ideas. Write these down in your journal.

3. Identify and locate six people your age (three males and three females) and six people (three males and three females) who are about ten to twenty years older (or younger) that you feel will be open and honest with you about their experiences with sexual communication in dating.

4. In each interview:
   a) Assure the person that you are interviewing that his or her identity will not be revealed and that the interview will be used solely for the purpose of this assignment.
   b) Be sure to list the person's gender and their approximate age.
   c) Describe each scenario to the person. After each description, ask the following questions:
      - Have you ever been in a situation like that?
      - If yes, how did you react?
      - Why do you think you reacted the way you did?
      - If you have not been in a situation like that, how do you think you would react to it?
      - Why do you think you would react that way?

5. After you complete all of your interviews, summarize your results. See if you can determine any patterns of how people answered based upon their age and their gender.

Option: essay
Write an essay (about four to five pages) about whether (and, if so, how and why) issues of sexual communication in dating are related to gender and age, and, if so, why. To write your essay, use information from the interviews you conducted above (including quotes and summaries of the interviews) and material from the sections in Chapter 4 on sexual attitudes and behavior, sexual communication in dating, and traditional gender roles.

Option: bibliography
Use your library's indexes (eg., *Social Science Index, Sociological Abstracts*, and so on) to develop a bibliography of ten articles from sociology or other social science journals that deal with issues related to sexual communication in dating. You may have to look under a variety of topics to find appropriate sources. Try looking under dating and sex, sex and dating, date rape, token resistance, sexual communication, unwanted sex, and so on.

Option: research paper
Complete the above journal and bibliographic instructions if you have not already done so. Write a paper (around seven to nine pages, typed) in which you:

1. Briefly discuss issues of sexual communication in dating.

2. Briefly discuss your interviews (questions you asked, how you selected the people to be interviewed, problems that you had with the interviews, and so on).

3. Use information from **five** of the journal articles from the bibliography you developed and material from Chapter 4 of your textbook to write a paper about sexual communication in dating.

4. Be sure to provide proper documentation throughout the paper and include a reference page.

NOTES:

PROJECT 4. 2 Do Males and Females Love Differently?

Chapter 4 of your textbook discusses six love styles —eros, mania, agape, pragma, storge, and ludus—and also discusses research about how the love styles of men and women differ. In this project, you will conduct your own research on the love styles of men and women. The activity is based on a modified version of a questionnaire administered by Hendrick et al. (1984) in their study of love styles of men and women. This activity can be done by students individually, in groups, or as a class.

Instructions:

1. Select a sample of students at your college to whom you will administer the questionnaire that appears on the following pages. Here are a few possible ways that you can select your sample, but do not feel that you have to limit yourself to any of these.

a) Obtain a list of student's names and addresses at your school from the registrar's office and select a random sample of about one hundred students from that list. Make one hundred copies of the questionnaire that appears on the following page and send it to those students, along with a self addressed, stamped envelope. If you have access to campus mail, this will save considerable money. This will be expensive if you do this on your own, so if you choose this option you might want to work with other members of your class.

b) Ask a few of your professors if you can administer the questionnaire to their classes. Try to have at least one hundred students complete the questionnaire. Again, it will be costly to make copies of the questionnaire unless you work with other students.

c) **This is probably the most practical approach.** Administer the questionnaire to all of the students in your class. Students can use the questionnaire in their own study guides, tear them out, and turn them in. If more than one student in the class is doing this project, have your professor place the returned questionnaires on reserve in the library or in another place that the students working on the project can have access to.

2. Divide the returned questionnaires into two piles: males and females. Then calculate the mean (average) male score and female score for each item. Do this by adding up the circled number for each item and divide by the number of total responses. (Or if you know how, enter the scores for each question into a computer and generate the mean scores for males and females for each question.) For each question, then, you will end up with a mean male score and a mean female score.

3. Next, arrange the mean scores for males and for females into the following categories:

Eros	Items 1, 7, 17, 20, 23, 35, 41, 52, 54
Ludus	Items 6, 14, 15, 26, 27, 33, 34, 46
Storge	Items 2, 5, 8, 21, 29, 32, 37, 50, 51, 53
Pragma	Items 4, 9, 16, 28, 31, 38, 42, 47, 49
Mania	Items 3, 10, 11, 18, 22, 25, 39, 43, 45
Agape	Items 12, 13, 19, 24, 30, 36, 40, 44, 48

To arrange your answers, make tables similar to the following:

Love Style	**Item**	**Male Mean**	**Female Mean**
Eros	1	???	???
	7	???	???
	17	???	???
	20	???	???
	etc.		
Ludus	6	???	???
	14	???	???
	etc.		

etc.

4. Once you complete the table that compares male and female mean scores for each item, carefully examine the scores within each category. Remember, the lower the mean score, the greater the agreement with the item.

Option: essay

Write an essay (four to five pages) in which you discuss the results of the survey. Feel free to discuss whatever you think is important. Some things you might consider are: Which love styles are more likely to characterize each gender? Which items received the most agreement and most disagreement by males? By females? Why do you think the results turned out the way they did?

Option: bibliography

Generate a bibliography of five to ten articles from sociology journals and popular periodicals about the love styles of males and females. Chapter 4 of your textbook mentions a few. Use your library's index to find others.

Option: research paper

Write a paper (seven to nine pages) in which you use your survey data and information found in four of the articles in your bibliography to compare love styles for men and women. Some issues to address include: How do your survey results compare with what the articles say? If not, can you offer some possible explanations? What are the differences in love styles between males and females? What are some possible explanations for the differences in love styles between males and females? Chapter 4 of your textbook should provide you with a good start in finding answers to some of these questions.

NOTES:

Love Styles Survey

Instructions: Below are 54 items concerning your loving style. At the right of each question please circle the number which indicates your level of agreement with the item. Please answer as honestly as possible.
Strongly agree = 1, Agree = 2, Neutral = 3, Disagree = 4, Strongly disagree = 5.

Please indicate your gender.

Male _____
Female_____

	SA	A	N	D	SD
1. I believe that "love at first sight" is possible.	1	2	3	4	5
2. I did not realize that I was in love until I actually had been for some time.	1	2	3	4	5
3. When things aren't going right with us, my stomach gets upset.	1	2	3	4	5
4. From a practical point of view, I must consider what a person is going to become before I commit myself to loving him/her.	1	2	3	4	5
5. You cannot have love unless you first have *caring* for a while.	1	2	3	4	5
6. It's always a good idea to keep your lover a little uncertain about how committed you are to him/her.	1	2	3	4	5
7. The first time we kissed or rubbed cheeks, I felt a definite genital response (lubrication, erection).	1	2	3	4	5
8. I still have good friendships with almost everyone with whom I have ever been involved in a love relationship.	1	2	3	4	5
9. It makes good sense to plan your life carefully before you choose a lover.	1	2	3	4	5
10. When my love affairs break up, I get so depressed that I have even thought of suicide.	1	2	3	4	5
11. Sometimes I get so excited about being in love that I can't sleep.	1	2	3	4	5

	SA	A	N	D	SD
12. I try to use my own strength to help my lover through difficult times, even when he/she is behaving foolishly.	1	2	3	4	5
13. I would rather suffer myself than let my lover suffer.	1	2	3	4	5
14. Part of the fun of being in love is testing one's skill at keeping it going and getting what one wants from it at the same time.	1	2	3	4	5
15. As far as my lovers go, what they don't know won't hurt them.	1	2	3	4	5
16. It is best to love someone with a similar background.	1	2	3	4	5
17. We kissed each other soon after we met because we both wanted to.	1	2	3	4	5
18. When my lover doesn't pay attention to me, I feel sick all over.	1	2	3	4	5
19. I cannot be happy unless I place my lover's happiness before my own.	1	2	3	4	5
20. Usually the first thing that attracts my attention to a person is his/her pleasing physical appearance.	1	2	3	4	5
21. The best kind of love grows out of a long friendship.	1	2	3	4	5
22. When I am in love, I have trouble concentrating on anything else.	1	2	3	4	5
23. At the first touch of his/her hand, I knew that love was a real possibility.	1	2	3	4	5
24. When I break up with someone, I go out of my way to see that he/she is O.K.	1	2	3	4	5
25. I cannot relax if I suspect that he/she is with someone else.	1	2	3	4	5
26. I have at least once had to plan carefully to keep two of my lovers from finding out about each other.	1	2	3	4	5
27. I can get over love affairs pretty easily and quickly.	1	2	3	4	5
28. A main consideration in choosing a lover is how he/she reflects on my family.	1	2	3	4	5

	SA	A	N	D	SD
29. The best part of love is living together, building a home together, and rearing children together.	1	2	3	4	5
30. I am usually willing to sacrifice my own wishes to let my lover achieve his/hers.	1	2	3	4	5
31. A main consideration in choosing a partner is whether or not he/she will be a good parent.	1	2	3	4	5
32. Kissing, cuddling, and sex shouldn't be rushed into; they will happen naturally when one's intimacy has grown enough.	1	2	3	4	5
33. I enjoy flirting with attractive people.	1	2	3	4	5
34. My lover would get upset if he/she knew some of the things I've done with other people.	1	2	3	4	5
35. Before I ever fell in love, I had a pretty clear physical picture of what my true love would be like.	1	2	3	4	5
36. If my lover had a baby by someone else, I would want to raise it, love it, and care for it as if it were my own.	1	2	3	4	5
37. It is hard to say exactly when we fell in love.	1	2	3	4	5
38. I couldn't truly love anyone I would not be willing to marry.	1	2	3	4	5
39. Even though I don't want to be jealous, I can't help it when he/she pays attention to someone else.	1	2	3	4	5
40. I would rather break up with my lover than stand in his/her way.	1	2	3	4	5
41. I like the idea of my lover and myself having the same kinds of clothes, hats, plants, bicycles, cars. etc.	1	2	3	4	5
42. I wouldn't date anyone that I wouldn't want to fall in love with.	1	2	3	4	5
43. At least once when I thought a love affair was all over, I saw him/her again and knew I couldn't realistically see that person again without loving him/her.	1	2	3	4	5
44. Whatever I own is my lover's to use as he/she chooses.	1	2	3	4	5

	SA	A	N	D	SD
45. If my lover ignores me for a while, I sometimes do really stupid things to try to get his/her attention back.	1	2	3	4	5
46. It would be fun to see whether I can get someone to go out with me even if I don't want to get involved with that person.	1	2	3	4	5
47. A main consideration in choosing a mate is how he/she will reflect on one's career.	1	2	3	4	5
48. When my lover doesn't see me or call for a while, I assume he/she has a good reason.	1	2	3	4	5
49. Before getting very involved with anyone I try to figure out how compatible his/her hereditary background is with mine in case we ever have children.	1	2	3	4	5
50. The best love relationships are the ones that last the longest.	1	2	3	4	5
51. Love is really a deep friendship, not a mysterious, mystical emotion.	1	2	3	4	5
52. Strong physical attraction is one of the best aspects of being in love.	1	2	3	4	5
53. The most satisfying love relationships are those that develop between good friends.	1	2	3	4	5
54. I am delighted with the appearance of my lover.	1	2	3	4	5

NOTES:

CHAPTER 5

PATTERNS OF MATE CHOICE AND COHABITATION

CHAPTER OUTLINE

Theories of Mate Choice
- Exchange Theory
- Stimulus-Value-Role Theory
- Systems Theory

Patterns of Mate Selection
- The Marriage Squeeze
- Delayed Marriage
- Interracial Marriage

Cohabitation
- Who Are the Cohabitors?

Explanations for Cohabitation
- Cohabitation as Trial Marriage
- Cohabitation and Divorce
- The Marriage Disillusionment Explanation
- Cohabitation as Convenience
- American Cohabitation

NOTES:

CHAPTER LEARNING OBJECTIVES

After studying this chapter, you should be able to:

- identify three theories of mate choice;
- discuss and critique the exchange theory of mate choice;
- discuss and critique the stimulus-value-role theory of mate choice;
- discuss and critique the systems theory of mate choice;
- identify and discuss patterns of choice;
- discuss cohabitation trends in the United States and explanations for cohabitation.

KEY POINTS FOR REVIEW

- There are a number of theories of mate choice. According to exchange theory, the choice of a partner depends on the perception that the assets and liabilities of the partner are equivalent to one's own assets and liabilities. These assets and liabilities generally include things such as age, race, education, income or other items that people place a high value on. A criticism of exchange theory is that it views mate selection as rational, mechanical, and calculated, and overlooks the emotional aspects of romantic love and the interpersonal dynamics by which romantic attraction is developed.

- Like exchange theory, the stimulus-value-role theory maintains that people are drawn toward potential mates who have overall assets and liabilities equivalent to their own. In addition, though, the stimulus-value-role theory is a filter theory that holds that courtship involves a series of stages which begin with acquaintanceship and moves toward commitment. The stimulus stage is the physical attraction stage. The value stage is the stage in which the potential partners discuss their likes, dislikes, values and life goals. In the role stage, the partners determine if the actions of each other are compatible. A criticism of the stimulus-value-role theory is that the stages are not necessarily mutually exclusive, nor do they necessarily occur in the above order. It also assumes that mate selection is an overly rational process.

- Systems theory maintains that there is a connection between the social role which people play in their family of origin and the kind of mate they select. According to this view, there is a tendency for people to gravitate toward partners with whom they can reenact their childhood family roles. A criticism of systems theory is that most of its research has been conducted by therapists working in the treatment of substance abuse or mental illness and, thus, may result in overgeneralization to the general population.

• A marriage squeeze exists when one gender experiences a shortage of potential marriage partners of the appropriate marriage age. A marriage squeeze tends to occur when the birth rate is rising or falling. Women in America faced a marriage squeeze from the late 1950s to the 1980s. There will be a marriage squeeze for men until the turn of the century.

• It is becoming increasingly common for men and women to delay getting married until they are in their late twenties. Reasons for this include the changing job structure, the increase of women in the labor force, the sexual revolution, and the rising divorce rate.

• There were six times as many interracial marriages in the United States in 1990 than in 1960. The United States is moving from a pattern of racial endogamy—a tendency to marry within one's own race—to one in which racial exogamy—a tendency to marry outside of one's race—is becoming more prevalent.

• Cohabitation—two unmarried adults who are living together in a sexual relationship—has increased more than five-sfold since 1950. By age 30, over 40% of Americans have cohabitated at some time in their lives. Although all types of people cohabitate, cohabitors are typically white, urban, and lower income. Typical female cohabitors are single parents. Cohabitors are more likely than non-cohabitors to subscribe to non-traditional gender roles and tend to be less religious.

• There are a number of explanations for cohabitation between opposite sex partners. First, it may represent a cautious tendency to engage in trial marriage. From the functionalist perspective, cohabitation serves as a source of realism role adjustment, and freedom from childbearing pressure. The higher incidence of divorce for cohabitors suggests that cohabitation does not increase marital stability. A second explanation for cohabitation is that people have become disillusioned with marriage. People with traditional values are more likely to move directly to marriage without cohabiting. Third, some people cohabitate simply as a source of convenience, without any particular philosophy about marriage.

NOTES:

KEY TERMS

The following key terms are found in your textbook on the page number indicated in parentheses. In the space provided, write a brief definition of the key term. Then provide an example of the term, such as a culture in which the practice takes place, or people that you might know whose behavior illustrates the term. You could include issues that you might have read about in the news or in a book, or anything else that will illustrate the term and help you remember it. Include any comments from your class discussions or textbook that might help you remember and understand these key terms.

exchange theory of mate choice (p. 119)

____

____

____

field of eligibles (p. 116)

____

____

____

stimulus-value-role theory of mate choice (p. 120)

____

____

____

systems theory of mate choice (p. 122)

____

____

enabler or codependent (p. 124)

dysfunctional family (p. 124)

functional family (p. 124)

overgeneralization (p. 125)

marriage squeeze (p. 126)

first marriage (p. 128)

endogamy (p. 130)

racial endogamy (p. 130)

exogamy (p. 130)

racial exogamy (p. 130)

cohabitation (p. 132)

trial marriage (p. 133)

functionalism (p. 134)

NOTES:

PRACTICE TEST

Multiple Choice

1. Which theory (theories) of mate choice focus on the social assets and liabilities that each partner brings to the relationship?
   a) exchange theory only
   b) stimulus-value-role theory and exchange theory
   c) systems theory and exchange theory
   d) systems theory only

2. According to exchange theory, for a relationship to continue:
   a) each person feels that the overall assets and liabilities exchanged by the partners are roughly equivalent
   b) one partner feels he/she is enjoying a greater share of the assets
   c) one partner feels he/she is assuming more than an equal share of the liabilities
   d) both partners feel that they are being slighted

3. In traditional Mexican-American culture, the name of the "go-between" sent by the male's family to visit a prospective bride's family to convey the man's interest is the:
   a) mediator
   b) evaluator
   c) portador
   d) conquistador

4. The theory of mate choice which maintains that couples must pass through a series of "filtering" stages before becoming committed to each other is:
   a) exchange theory
   b) stimulus-value-role theory
   c) systems theory
   d) developmental theory

5. The theory of mate choice that says that people gravitate toward partners with whom they can reenact their childhood family roles is:
   a) exchange theory
   b) stimulus-value-role theory
   c) systems theory
   d) developmental theory

6. In a test of exchange theory, researchers Schoen and Wooldrige found that:
   a) white men tended to marry younger, less educated women
   b) white men tended to marry younger women who had an equivalent or higher education
   c) African American women tended to marry more educated African American men
   d) African American men tended to marry younger, less educated white women

7. An important criticism of the exchange theory of mate choice is that:
   a) it places too much emphasis on romance
   b) it places the interpersonal dynamics of a relationship as more central than practical matters
   c) it overlooks the emotional aspects of romantic love
   do) it focuses more on explaining mate selection patterns of males than females

8. A criticism of the stimulus-value-role theory of mate choice is that:
   a) life is not necessarily equivalent to a stage, as Goffman has suggested in the dramaturgical perspective
   b) it assumes that people place too much emphasis on the stage in which commitment finally occurs
   c) the stages do not necessarily follow the order suggested in the theory
   d) it assumes that there is an underlying tendency for romance on the part of people

9. A criticism of the systems theory of mate choice is that:
   a) it assumes that families are social systems
   b) it assumes that mate choice is a rational process
   c) it overgeneralizes the possibility that mate choice operates on a low level of consciousness
   d) it assumes that people have an innate desire for romance

10. According to systems theory, "dysfunctional families," in contrast to "functional families" exhibit:
    a) flexible social roles
    b) lack of social roles
    c) too many social roles
    d) rigid social roles

11. A marriage squeeze exists:
    a) when people begin to feel pressure to get married due to their increasing age
    b) when one gender experiences a shortage of potential marriage partners of the appropriate marriage age
    c) when a couple successfully passes through the filtering process
    d) during the first two years of marriage

12. Since 1970, the proportion of women age 25 to 29 who have never married:
a) has been reduced by half
b) has doubled
c) has tripled
d) has remained about the same, but is likely to decline by the turn of the century

13. In 1990, the median age for first marriage was:
a) 19.8 for women and 22.5 for men
b) 23.9 for women and 26.1 for men
c) 27.3 for women and 30.1 for men
d) 26.1 for women and 23.9 for men

14. In the United States, interracial marriage:
a) increased during the 1960s, but has once again declined
b) has been declining since the passage of the Civil Rights Act
c) has not changed much over the past three decades, despite changes in the family
d) occurs six time more often than it did in the 1960s

15. The cultural tendency to marry someone from your own social group (race, income, and so on) is called:
a) endogamy
b) exogamy
c) homogamy
d) heterogamy

16. The cultural tendency to marry someone from a race other than your own is called:
a) cultural relativism
b) racio-marital adversity
c) racial homogamy
d) racial exogamy

17. A number of studies have found that cohabitors typically:
a) are African Americans with low incomes
b) are single females with no children
c) subscribe to non-traditional gender roles
d) are very traditional in their views about sexuality, despite their cohabitation

18. According to functionalist perspectives, cohabitation:
a) provides an opportunity for important developmental tasks to take place prior to marriage
b) creates a source of conflict between the partners that eventually undermines the marriage
c) stems from an unconscious desire to resolve childhood issues
d) lowers the marriage rate and thus serves to control overpopulation

19. Studies of cohabitation suggest that people who cohabitate:
    a) tend to have more stable, well adjusted marriages
    b) have marriages that are no more or less stable than people who did not cohabitate before marriage
    c) have a higher divorce rate than people who not cohabitate before marriage
    d) none of the above

20. Which of the following is NOT generally recognized by social scientists as an explanation for the increase in cohabitation?
    a) it is a form of trial marriage
    b) it represents disillusionment with marriage
    c) it is a matter of convenience
    d) it alleviates guilt about pre-marital sex

NOTES:

PROJECTS

PROJECT 5. 1 Who Will Your Spouse Be?

Do you ever wonder what your spouse will be like? What will he or she look Like? Will he or she be intelligent? What religion will he or she be? Will he or she have a good job? And so on. You probably know a great deal more about what your spouse will be like than you realize. This is because there are particular social and cultural factors that influence our choice of spouse. Many of us like to fantasize that our choice of marriage partner results from some type of non-rational attraction to another that we have no conscious control over. This may be the case in some instances. But usually, our choices of marriage partners are less likely to be attributed to chance and chemistry than to rational choice. The objectives of this project are to have you examine and understand the social and cultural forces surrounding how we select a spouse, and to have you examine the sociological theories, concepts, and ideas pertaining to mate selection.

Journal instructions:

1. Reread the sections in Chapter five on theories of mate choice and patterns of mate selection. In your journal, list, take notes on, and summarize the theories, concepts, and ideas that help to explain the ways in which people choose mates and the patterns of mate selection.

2. React to each of the above theories, concepts, and ideas that you have written about in your journal. Do you agree or disagree with them? Why? Which ones are particularly meaningful to you or relevant to you? How might they pertain to your life? And so on.

3. Based upon your culture's and family's norms regarding choice of marriage partner and the above theories, concepts, and ideas, make a list of characteristics that you would probably not consider, would be prohibited or discouraged from considering, or would not have the opportunity to consider for a marriage partner. Consider the following characteristics, or others that you can think of: age, gender, race, religion, ethnicity, education, political values, beliefs, social class, physical appearance, education, and so on.

4. Examine each of the characteristics of marriage partners that you have eliminated. In your journal, briefly explain the social forces that led you to eliminate each of those characteristics. Discuss any relevant theories, concepts, or ideas about mate choice or patterns of mate selection that might help you explain why people with these characteristics might be eliminated.

5. Now that you know who you are not likely to marry, list the possibilities of each characertistic that you would consider, would be allowed to consider, and would have the opportunity to meet someone with that characteristic. Again, once you have done this, examine the list in terms of theories, concepts, and ideas about mate choice and patterns of mate selection discussed in Chapter five.

Option: essay

Use your sociological knowledge of theories of mate choice and patterns of mate selection, and your above journal reflections to write a scenario (around three to five pages, typed) in which you discuss where you might be likely to meet your spouse, what types of characteristics he or she is likely to have, how you come to realize that this person might be a potential spouse, how various social and cultural forces might influence the suitability of this person as a potential spouse, and so on. Make sure that your essay has a basis in the theories, concepts, and ideas about mate choice and mate selection found in Chapter five. Take your time, be creative, and have fun with this one. You will enjoy reading it again some time in the future.

PROJECT 5. 2 Endogamy and Exogamy as Cultural Factors in Dating and Mate Choice

There have been a number of movies made that have dealt with issues of endogamy and exogamy in dating and in mate choice. For example, *Guess Who's Coming to Dinner*, produced in the 1960s, and *Jungle Fever*, produced in the early 1990s, deal with issues related to racial endogamy and exogamy. *The Graduate*, produced in the 1960s, and *Harold and Maud,* produced in the early 1970s, deal with issues regarding age endogamy and exogamy. Other movies deal with class endogamy and exogamy, such as *Romeo and Juliet*. There are dozens of other movies that deal with issues related to endogamy and exogamy in dating and mate choice. The objective of this assignment is to have you gain insight about the extent to which endogamy or exogamy are important cultural factors in dating and mate choice and why.

Journal instructions:

1. Obtain a movie from your college library, local library, or video store that deals with issues of endogamy and exogamy. Any of the above movies are suitable, but there are others also that you may wish to use. Before completing this assignment, check with your professor if the movie that you have selected is suitable for this project.

2. View the movie that you have selected and pay close attention to all of the issues related to endogamy and exogamy that occur in the movie. Discuss, in detail, each of these in your journal.

3. Interview three people who are involved (either dating or married) to someone outside of their racial, age, social class, ethnic, religious, educational, or other important social group. Ask them about what issues they face with each other and within society that stem from being intimately involved in an exogamous relationship.

Option: essay

Write a three to five page essay (typed) in which you discuss why marrying outside of one's racial, age, ethnic, income, religious, educational and other important groups may be problematic and hy it tends to be stigmatized within American culture. Use material from the movie you viewed and your journal notes (above) to illustrate your points and discuss your ideas.

Option: bibliography

Using your library's indexes, develop a bibliography of ten articles about endogamy and exogamy in dating and marriage. Articles about interracial and interfaith marriages should be fairly easy to locate, but see if you can find articles about other types of exogamous relationships also. Make sure that at least five of the articles in your bibliography are from social science journals. Type your bibliography using the format found in your textbook or in the social science journals.

Option: research paper
Write a paper (around five to seven pages, typed) in which you integrate ideas that you discussed in your journal (above) with material from five articles in your bibliography to discuss whether or not you feel that endogamy is an important cultural norm. Support your position with information found in the articles you select, the movie you viewed, the interviews you conducted, and ideas from your textbook. Be sure to provide proper documentation for all sources that you use and include a reference (works cited) page.

CHAPTER 6

SEXUALITY

CHAPTER OUTLINE

The Human Sexual Response
- Excitement
- Plateau
- Orgasm
- Resolution

The Use of Contraception
- Race, Ethnicity, and Social Class
- Stage in Dating
- Marriage and Contraception

Sexuality in Marriage and Midlife
- Sexual Initiations
- Outlook on Life and Sexual Satisfaction
- Gender Differences in Sexuality
- Sexual Disenchantment
- Sexual Fantasies

Extramarital Sexual Affairs
- Gender Differences in Extramarital Sex
- Relationship with the Extramarital Partner
- Motivation for Extramarital Sexual Affairs
- Extramarital Sexual and Emotional Affairs

Same-Sex Relationships
- Gay Male Relationships
- Female Lesbian Relationships

Alcohol, Drugs, and Sex
- Alcohol, Drugs, and the Onset of Sexual Intercourse

Sexually Transmitted Diseases
- Men, Women, and Sexually Transmitted Diseases

Acquired Immune Deficiency Syndrome

- What is AIDS?
- Latency Period
- AIDS Related Complex
- Incidence
- HIV Transmission
- Growing Heterosexual Transmission
- Homosexual Transmission
- HIV and Other STDs
- High-Risk Sexual Behavior
- AIDS in Men and Women

CHAPTER LEARNING OBJECTIVES

After studying this chapter, you should be able to:

- identify and fully describe the levels of the human sexual response;
- identify and discuss patterns of contraceptive use among different social groups, in dating, and in marriage;
- discuss the areas of sexuality in marriage including sexual initiation, sexual satisfaction, gender differences in sexuality, sexual disenchantment, and sexual fantasies;
- discuss extramarital sexual affairs with regard to frequency at which they occur, gender differences, relationships with the extramarital partner, motivations for affairs, and differences between sexual affairs and emotional affairs;
- discuss the extent to which same-sex relationships exist and the differences between gay male and female lesbian relationships;
- discuss the relationship between alcohol, drugs, and sex;
- discuss the characteristics of AIDS, its incidence, ways in which it is transmitted, its patterns among homosexuals, heterosexuals, men, and women, and its relationship with other STDs.

KEY POINTS FOR REVIEW

• Masters and Johnson identified four phases of the human sexual response: excitement, plateau, orgasm, and resolution. In the excitement stage the person experiences increasing sexual arousal. In the plateau stage, the body prepares for orgasm. In the orgasm stage, sexual tension rises to a peak and is discharged. In the resolution stage, sexual intensity gradually subsides and muscle tension is replaced by relaxation.

• Most people do not plan for contraceptive use during their first sexual encounter and half of all women do not use contraceptives at their first experiences of pre-marital sexual intercourse. Contraceptive use at first intercourse differs by race, ethnicity, and social class.

• People with high levels of sex guilt are least likely to use contraceptives at first intercourse. In non-monogomous relationships, the condom is usually the contraceptive most chosen. This tends to change to the birth control pill when the relationship becomes monogamous. The most common form of birth control in married couples is surgical sterilization of one of the partners. The second most often used contraceptive for married couples is the birth control pill.

• In general, married men initiate sex more often than married women. Women restrict sexual activity more often than men. The main reasons for restricting sexual activity include fatigue and lack of time.

• Husband and wives who believe that their life has a purpose tend to have a satisfying sex life. Partners who are overly concerned with their own sexual arousal tend to be dissatisfied with their sex lives.

• There are important differences in sexuality for married men and women. For men, a frequent complain is that sex does not occur often enough. Men tend to equate lack of sex with rejection by their partner. The most common sexual complain of women is inadequate amount of sexual foreplay and not enough "afterglow" time. Women tend to have a more sensuous focus whereas men tend to have an orgasm focus.

• Even though most married couples report a satisfying sex life, some complain of sexual disenchantment in which passion and excitement go out of sex. Some reasons for sexual disenchantment include the decline of intense love, stress, and habituation.

• Both men and women fantasize about sexual situations. The most frequent sexual fantasies of both men and women include cunnilingus and fellatio. Next are fantasies about having sex with a famous person, and having sex with multiple partners.

• In the Unites States, from one-third to one-half of married people have had an extramarital sexual affair. The incidence of extramarital sex has been on the rise over the past forty years, but the trend now appears to be reversing.

• There are important gender differences with regard to extramarital sexual affairs. Men have extramarital sex earlier in marriage and more often. Women are more likely than men to become emotionally involved with their extramarital sexual partner.

• Some reasons for extramarital sexual affairs include the desire to seek romance, sexual curiosity, the desire to avoid intimacy in marriage, deprivation in marriage, and self development.

• Approximately four percent of males and females are homosexual or bisexual. There are four types of gay male relationships. First, some gay men have no special lover living with them. Second, some have a regular lover, but live separately. Third, those in a closed-couple relationship practice sexual exclusivity with their lover. Fourth, some have an open-couple relationship in which sexuality is not exclusive.

• Lesbians tend to be more emotionally involved with their lovers than gay men are. Most lesbian relationships are egalitarian, rather than as they are stereotypically perceived as having dominant-submissive roles. Lesbians engage in less sexual activity than heterosexuals or gay males.

• High-risk sexual behavior and the onset of sexual activity of college students and young adolescents is directly related to the use of alcohol or illicit drugs.

• Sexually transmitted diseases (STDs) are infections that generally affect the genital area or the soft tissue of the mouth. Fear of contracting a STD has not reduced sexual activity. While STDs are a concern for both men and women, they pose a particularly serious problem for women because warning symptoms do not appear as readily among women. One STD that has no early symptoms in men or women is HIV which leads to AIDS.

• HIV causes AIDS by attacking critical cells in the immune system, thus making the body more vulnerable to opportunistic diseases—diseases which the body normally has some resistance. HIV has been called the "invisible epidemic" because after becoming infected with HIV there may be a latency period of ten years in which no symptoms occur yet the virus can still be transmitted. AIDS Related Complex (ARC)—night sweats, inexplicable weight loss, swollen lymph nodes, fatigue, fever, chills, chronic diarrhea and other flu-like symptoms—usually appears before the onset of full-blown AIDS.

• HIV is a world-wide epidemic that has infected over twelve million people. Over two million people have already died of AIDS. In the United States, over one million people have been infected with HIV, there are over 300,000 AIDS cases of which over 150,000 people already have died.

• HIV is not transmitted through casual social contact, but occurs when the body fluids or the body tissue of an infected person come into contact with the blood system of an uninfected person. This most commonly occurs through sharing HIV contaminated needles among intravenous drug users, anal or vaginal intercourse, and transmission from mother to fetus during pregnancy. Although the two largest categories of AIDS cases in the United States are homosexual males and intravenous drug users, HIV is primarily a heterosexually transmitted disease worldwide. Worldwide, one-third of AIDS cases are women who acquired the disease heterosexually.

• Many people still make the erroneous assumption that they do not have to worry about contracting HIV if they are not in one of the two major high risk groups (gay males and intravenous drug users). The sexual transmission of HIV in the heterosexual population is rapidly increasing. The fastest growing category of AIDS patients in the United States today is women who have acquired HIV through heterosexual intercourse. HIV is more efficiently transmitted from men to women during sexual intercourse than the other way around.

• Lesbian women have less exposure to HIV than gay men. Gay men are at high risk for contracting HIV because of multiple partners and anal intercourse. The spread of AIDS among homosexuals has fueled homophobia—the fear and hatred of homosexuals.

• People infected with HIV makes them more susceptible to other STDs such as herpes and syphilis. Further, once the HIV virus enters a homosexual or heterosexual population, high-risk sexual behavior—having sex with a stranger, or casual acquaintance, multiple sex partners, sex with a person who is at high-risk for AIDS, and vaginal or anal intercourse without a condom—exposes others to the possibility of contracting the infection.

• The two most common opportunistic diseases associated with AIDS in men are Kaposi's sarcoma—a deadly form of skin cancer—and pneumocystic pneumonia—a disease which eventually causes respiratory failure. These occur less often in women infected with HIV. For women, the most common ailments associated with AIDS are chronic vaginal yeast infections, throat yeast infections (thrush), and invasive cervical cancer.

NOTES:

KEY TERMS

The following key terms are found in your textbook on the page number indicated in parentheses. In the space provided, write a brief definition of the key term. Then provide an example of the term, such as a culture in which the practice takes place, or people that you might know whose behavior illustrates the term. You could include issues that you might have read about in the news or in a book, or anything else that will illustrate the term and help you remember it. Include any comments from your class discussions or textbook that might help you remember and understand these key terms.

excitement stage (p. 143)

____

____

____

vasocongestion (p. 143)

____

____

____

clitoris (p. 143)

____

____

____

pre-ejaculatory fluid (p. 143)

____

____

neuromuscular tension (p. 144)

orgasmic platform (p. 145)

clitoral hood (p. 145)

sex flush (p. 145)

labia (p. 143)

plateau stage (p. 144)

orgasm stage (p. 145)

resolution stage (p. 145)

refractory period (p. 145)

sexual disenchantment (p. 152)

novelty effect (p. 152)

cunnilingus (p. 153)

fellatio (p. 153)

sexual orientation (p. 155)

closed-coupled (p. 156)

open-coupled (p. 156)

high-risk sexual behavior (p. 165)

asymptomatic (p. 161)

AIDS (p. 161)

HIV (p. 161)

retrovirus (p. 161)

opportunistic diseases (p. 161)

latency period (p. 162)

ARC (p. 162)

pandemic (p. 162)

AIDS-worry (p. 165)

homophobia (p. 165)

Kaposi's sarcoma (p. 166)

NOTES:

PRACTICE TEST

Multiple Choice

1. According to Masters and Johnson, when having sex the first physiological changes occur:
   a) during the excitement stage for men, and during the plateau stage for women
   b) during the plateau stage for both men and women
   c) during the plateau stage for men, and during the excitement stage for women
   d) during the excitement stage for both men and women

2. The onset of vaginal lubrication:
   a) can occur at a low level of sexual arousal
   b) occurs only when the woman is ready for intercourse and near orgasm
   c) occurs only during orgasm
   d) first occurs in the resolution stage

3. A man's erection:
   a) begins in the excitement stage and steadily increases until he reaches orgasm
   b) may diminish for a period of time, even though sexual arousal is still building to the plateau stage
   c) usually first occurs in the plateau stage
   d) begins during the excitement stage and reaches its full potential during the plateau stage

4. What percentage of women reported using no form of contraception during their first experience with pre-marital sexual intercourse?
   a) 10%
   b) 20%
   c) 50%
   d) 90%

5. People who feel guilty about having sex:
   a) are more likely to plan ahead for contraceptives than people who do not feel sex-guilt
   b) are less likely to plan ahead for contraceptives than people who do not feel sex-guilt
   c) are more likely to plan to use condoms than people who do not feel sex-guilt
   d) are no different in their use of contraceptives than people who do not feel sex-guilt

6. Who is most likely to use contraceptives at first intercourse?:
   a) Hispanic women
   b) African-American women
   c) Oriental women
   d) Jewish women

7. The most common form of birth control among married partners is:
   a) the condom
   b) the birth control pill
   c) withdrawal
   d) surgical sterilization

8. During marriage, as people age:
   a) their frequency of intercourse tends to decrease, and their sexual satisfaction tends to increase
   b) their frequency of intercourse tends to decrease, and sexual satisfaction tends to decrease
   c) their frequency of intercourse tends to increase, and their sexual satisfaction tends to decrease
   d) their frequency of intercourse tends to increase, and their sexual satisfaction tends to increase

9. People who are overly focused on their own sexual arousal tend:
   a) to be much more satisfied with their sex lives
   b) to know how to satisfy their partners
   c) to be dissatisfied with marital sex
   d) to have more intense orgasms

10. Which of the following is called the "anti-aphrodisiac"?
    a) the decline of intense love
    b) stress
    c) habituation
    d) bad oysters

11. One difference between men and women's extramarital sexual behavior is:
    a) men engage in extramarital sex earlier in marriage, but have fewer extramarital sexual partners than women
    b) men engage in extramarital sex earlier in marriage and have more extramarital sexual partners than women
    c) men tend to like their extramarital sexual lovers better than they like their wives, whereas women tend to like their husbands better than their extramarital lovers
    d) women tend to see extramarital sexual affairs as a way to improve their relationships with their husbands, whereas men see them primarily as a way to enhance their sex lives

12. In their book The Second Shift, Hochschild and Machung argue that tension in sexual relationships often occurs:
a) when one or both of the married partners have to work overtime to meet the financial needs of the family
b) when wives have to juggle employment and family responsibilities
c) when husbands feel pressure to gain extra income as a result of traditional gender role expectations
d) when either one of the married partners is having an extramarital sexual or emotional affair

13. According to social science research, which of the following is generally NOT considered a motivation for having an extramarital sexual affair?
a) sexual curiosity
b) self-development
c) decline in morals and values
d) avoiding intimacy with one's spouse

14. The percentage of male and female students at a southern California university who identified themselves as homosexual or bisexual is:
a) 40%
b) 20%
c) 14%
d) 4%

15. Closed-coupled gay male relationships:
a) are declining in favor of non-exclusive relationships
b) have always been the most predominant form of gay male relationship
c) are becoming more popular among gay males
d) have virtually become nonexistent for gay males

16. The typical role relationship that now exists among lesbians is:
a) one in which there is a dominant-submissive role relationship similar to traditional male-female relationships
b) one in which egalitarian role relationships are becoming the norm
c) one in which both partners attempt to be submissive
d) one in which egalitarianism is declining

17. That people who use alcohol or illicit drugs are more likely than non-users to engage in high-risk sexual behavior is true of:
a) gay men, but not lesbian women
b) heterosexuals but not homosexuals
c) homosexuals but not heterosexuals
d) all people

18. Sexually transmitted diseases are a concern for both men and women but:
a) pose a particularly serious problem for women because women are less likely to use birth control devices that inhibit the spread of STDs
b) pose a particularly serious problem for women because their symptoms are more likely to go undetected
c) pose a particularly serious problem for men because their symptoms are more likely to go undetected
d) pose a particularly serious problem for men because the male anatomy and physiology make them more susceptible to STDs

19. In the United States, the first two large groups to become infected with HIV and to be identified were:
a) homosexual males and intravenous drug users
b) homosexual males and females
c) homosexual females and intravenous drug users
d) heterosexual males and intravenous drug users

20. On a worldwide scale, HIV is primarily transmitted:
a) through homosexual males
b) through homosexual females
c) through heterosexual contact
d) through intravenous drug users

21. Today, the fastest growing category of AIDS patients in the United States is:
a) males who have acquired HIV through intravenous drug use
b) women who have acquired HIV through heterosexual intercourse
c) males who have acquired HIV through homosexual intercourse
d) females who have acquired HIV through intravenous drug use

22. A number of studies have found that those who were at high risk for acquiring an HIV infection:
a) were much more likely to use condoms than those who are not at high risk
b) were not very likely to use safer sex practices
c) were more likely to use condoms, but not limit their number of sexual partners
d) were more likely to limit their number of sexual partners

23. When an HIV-infected man's immune system begins to fail, the two most common opportunistic diseases that produce an AIDS diagnosis are:
a) prostate cancer and tuberculosis
b) Kaposi's sarcoma (a deadly form of skin cancer) and pneumocystic pneumonia
c) influenza and genital herpes
d) lung cancer and hepatitis

24. The spread of AIDS among homosexuals has led to:
a) greater compassion for homosexuals
b) increased fear and hatred of homosexuals
c) more job opportunities for homosexuals
d) better health insurance for homosexuals

25. Following infection with HIV, the latency period before AIDS develops lasts an average of:
a) one year
b) five years
c) ten years
d) fifteen years

PROJECTS

PROJECT 6. 1 Safer Sex Practices and Contraception Among College Students

It is no longer news that HIV, the virus that leads to AIDS, is spreading rapidly. What may, perhaps, be news to some people is that they it is now spreading at an alarming rate among heterosexuals. Yet, in spite of our knowledge about the spread of HIV, many people still neglect to practice safer sex. This project is intended to help you become more aware of the extent to which people are practicing safer sex and using contraceptives, and help you become more aware of the importance of practicing safe sex and using contraceptives.

Journal instructions:

1. Re-read Box 6. 6 in Chapter six of your textbook. In your journal, make a list of the safer sex practices listed in the box. After each, discuss how likely you have been in the past (if you have ever been sexually active), are currently, (if you are sexually active), or would be (if you are not sexually active) to engage in the safer sex practice. After each safer sex practice that you do not always follow (or have not, or are not likely to), discuss why.

2. Re-read the sections in chapter six about contraceptive techniques and Table 6.1. In your journal, make a list of contraceptive techniques and after each discuss how likely you have been in the past, are currently, or would be to engage that type of contraception. After each, discuss why or why not.

3. After you have examined your own practices with regards to engaging in safer sex and using contraception, conduct a survey of students at your college. You can do this on your own or you may choose to work with others in the class who are doing this project. Obtain a sample of about one hundred students to participate in your survey. A random sample is best, but if that is not possible or practical, use a convenience sample that may be available (various classes, residence halls, meeting places such as the cafeteria, campus center, library, or others). You can design your own survey, or use the one on the following page. If you wish, you can modify the questionnaire on the following page to include additional questions, or you can modify it to conduct a survey on either safer sex practices or contraceptive use.

4. Summarize the results of your questionnaire responses. Then answer the following questions about sexual practices at your college:
   a) Would you say that people who are sexually active at your college generally practice safer sex?
   b) Of the people who do not always practice safer sex, what types of unsafe sexual activity are most common?

c) Are there any differences in safer sex practices according to age, race, religion, gender and class?
d) Would you say that people who are sexually active at your college generally use contraceptives?
e) What types of contraceptives are used more often? Least often?
f) Are there any differences in contraceptive use according to age, race, religion, gender, and class?

Option: essay
Write an essay (around five pages, typed) in which you use the results of the above survey to discuss safer sex and contraceptive practices among students at your college and compare the results of the survey with relevant material about sex practices found in Chapter 6. Be sure to integrate comments made on the questionnaires.

Option: research paper
Obtain five articles about sex practices of young adults and college students from social science journals. Use information from these articles and the results of the above research to write a paper (around seven pages, typed) about safer sex practices and contraceptive use of young adults and college students. Be sure to provide proper documentation of your sources throughout the paper and include a reference (works cited) page.

Safer Sex and Contraceptive Practices Among College Students Survey

This survey is being conducted for a class on Marriage and the Family. The purpose of this survey is to determine the extent to which college students practice safer sex and to find out which types of contraceptives they use when they are sexually active. Your answers will be kept strictly confidential and you will remain anonymous. Thank-you for your cooperation.

1. Age ____16-18 ____19-21 ____21-23 ____24 and above

2. Race ______________________

3. Religion ______________________(if none, please say "none")

4. Gender ____Male ____Female

5. Class ____Freshmen ____Sophomore ____Junior ____Senior

6. Have you been sexually active (that is, have engaged in intercourse, oral sex, or other forms of intimate sexual activity with another person) within the past five years?
____Yes ____No

If you checked "yes," please answer the remainder of this questionnaire. If you checked "no," do not answer the remainder of the questionnaire and please wait patiently until the questionnaires are collected

7. When sexually active, how likely are you to:

	Always	Often	Sometimes	Never
• discuss safer sex practices with your partner?	____	____	____	____
• use a condom?	____	____	____	____
• use nonoxynol-9?	____	____	____	____
• avoid anal sex	____	____	____	____
• avoid multiple sex partners	____	____	____	____

• avoid casual sex	____	____	____	____
• avoid drug use	____	____	____	____
• require the partner to have an AIDS test	____	____	____	____

8. When sexually active, how likely are you (or your partner) to use the following methods of contraception?:

	Very likely	Somewhat likely	Not very likely	Never
• birth control pill	____	____	____	____
• IUD	____	____	____	____
• diaphragm	____	____	____	____
• condom	____	____	____	____
• spermicidal foam	____	____	____	____
• rhythm	____	____	____	____
• withdrawal	____	____	____	____
• surgical sterilization	____	____	____	____
• other methods (fill in)____________________	____	____	____	

9. If there are any safer sex practices that you do not <u>always</u> follow (items listed in question 7), please comment as to why not.

____

____

____

____

10. Please comment on why you use the types of contraceptive devices that you indicated that you are likely or very likely to use.

PROJECT 6. 2 AIDS-Related Social Issues

AIDS is spreading at rates which continuously surpass previous projections. At the time of this writing, over 300,000 Americans have been diagnosed with AIDS and over one million people have been infected with HIV. The World Health Organization (WHO) estimates the total cases of AIDS worldwide to be greater than 1.5 million, with eight to ten million people infected with HIV. The rapid spread of AIDS has led to a number of important related social issues, especially relevant to sex practices. For example: Should condoms be distributed upon request in schools? Should there be sex education in schools? If so, at what age (or grade) should sex education begin? Should "safer sex" education be a part of sex education programs? Should health-care practitioners (physicians, nurses, chiropractors, dentists, and so on) who have AIDS be allowed to continue to practice? Should health care-practitioners be required to treat AIDS sufferers? There are many other questions. The purpose of this project is to help you become aware of the social consequences of AIDS, especially as they relate to all of our family and personal lives.

Journal instructions:

I. Identify as many AIDS-related issues as you can that have occurred in the news over the past five years. You do not have to go through every newspaper and magazine to do this. Rather, you can probably do this effectively by looking through a sample of months in the various periodical and news indexes in your college library or local library (for example, *Reader's Guide to Periodical Literature, Social Science Index, New York Times Index, Newsbank,* and so on). Try to obtain fifteen to twenty articles that discuss a variety of the above issues or other issues related to AIDS. Pay particular attention to any issues that pertain to marriage and the family.

2. In your journal, make a list of the issues for which you found articles, and list all the articles (authors, dates, publication) that pertain to each issue. Use the articles to briefly summarize what each of the issues is about.

3. Use these issues to think about and discuss in your journal what the social consequences of AIDS may be, especially with regard to marriage and families. For example, what impact might early childhood sex education have on the types of relationships that people form at different stages in their life? How will the need to practice safer sex affect marriage rates and the ages at which people marry? How will the increasing rate of HIV and AIDS affect health insurance policies and the amount of money that families have to spend? There are many other issues related to AIDS. Try not to take a position for or against a policy or an issue. Rather, try to think of all the possible consequences—positive and negative—that each issue raises.

Option: essay

Using the material that you compiled in your journal (above) write an essay (around three to five pages, typed) in which you discuss how you think dating, marriage, and family life will change as a result of the AIDS epidemic. Carefully think about how each of the above issues that you identified might affect dating, marriage, and the family in the long run.

Option: research paper

Conduct further library research to find five or six articles from social science journals (not popular periodicals) and/or books written by social scientists (sociologists, psychologists, anthropologists, political scientists, public administrators, economists, and historians) that discuss the social consequences of AIDS. Write a paper (around five to seven pages, typed) in which you present an overview of the social consequences of AIDS from the point of view of social scientists, and use the issues you identified in your work above to illustrate what these consequences might be. Be sure to provide proper documentation throughout your paper and include a reference (works cited) page.

CHAPTER 7

MARRIAGE AND PARTNERSHIPS: INTERPERSONAL RELATIONSHIPS

CHAPTER OUTLINE

Marital Quality
- Family Ritual
- Spending Time Together
- Positive Communication Patterns
- Self-Revelation
- Intimacy
- Commitment
- Religious Beliefs

Marriage and Well-Being
- The Selection Hypothesis
- The Protection Hypothesis

Trends in Marital Happiness
- The Happiness Gap

Gender and Marital Interaction
- Breadth of Self-Revelation
- Empathy
- Gender, Marital Roles, and the Ideal Self

Marital Stances and Marital Distress
- Four Common Marital Stances
- Marital Stances Associated With Substance Abuse

Marriage Over the Life Cycle
- Declining Marital Satisfaction in the Parenting Years
- Comparing Parents to Non-parents
- Gender Differences in the Childbearing Years

Delayed Childbearers
Launching Children
Caregiving in Old Age
Illness and Death of a Spouse

Same-Sex Partnerships
Changing Legal Rights
Social Norms and Same-Sex Relationships
Commitment
Extended Kin

CHAPTER LEARNING OBJECTIVES

After studying this chapter, you should be able to:

- identify and discuss the factors associated with marital quality;
- discuss the relationship between marriage and personal well-being;
- discuss trends in marital happiness;
- discuss the ways in which gender affects marital interaction, especially in regard to self-revelation, empathy, and marital roles;
- identify and discuss four common stances taken by marriage partners that often arise in stressful situations;
- identify and discuss the marital stances taken when one spouse is chemically dependent;
- discuss the ways in which childbearing affects marital satisfaction and reasons why;
- discuss the ways in which marital satisfaction is affected during old age;
- discuss the legality of same-sex partnerships with regard to marriage, the future outlook for same-sex marriages, and some current legal problems with regard to same sex partnerships;
- discuss the characteristics of same-sex relationships in terms of ways in which gender roles are enacted, equality, level of commitment, relationships with extended kin, and integration into the gay world.

KEY POINTS FOR REVIEW

• Marital success refers to a marriage that lasts and has a high level of quality. There are a number of factors associated with marital quality (or marital satisfaction). These include family rituals (including cultural rituals such as religious holidays, and private rituals such as going out for pizza on Sunday nights), spending time together, positive communication patterns (such as discussing issues instead of personalities and avoiding cross-complaining), self-revelation, intimacy, commitment, and religious beliefs.

• Marital satisfaction tends to be high when the partners engage in similar amounts of self-revelation. Marital satisfaction also tends to be higher with moderate amounts of self-revelation. Marital satisfaction tends to be very low when very little self-revelation takes place, then rises as self-revelation increases. However, there is a point of dimishing returns. When self-revelation is extremely high, marital satisfaction tends to decrease.

• Married people generally have greater longevity and are more emotionally and physically healthy than those who are single. There are two explanations for this. The selection hypothesis argues that marriage and well-being are related because healthier people are selected into marriage. The protection hypothesis holds that marriage provides some important protections against emotional and physical illness.

• Although married people tend to be happier and more content with life than single people, the happiness gap—the greater happiness of married people than single people—is decreasing. The happiness gap between married and single women had diminished substantially between 1972 and 1989. This is due to greater happiness of single women and the added marital stress of employment on young married women. The happiness gap between married and single men also decreased during this period, but by a smaller amount than experienced by women.

• Socialization into traditional male and female gender roles influence how the husband and wife roles are enacted and how husbands and wives interact with each other. Different levels of self-revelation often makes it difficult for husbands and wives to communicate with each other. Wives typically provide a greater breadth of self-revelation than husbands. Likewise, men in the traditional male role tend to have a difficult time imagining how their wives feel.

• Gender role socialization help to create an image of an ideal self for us as males and females. These ideal self images influence people through guilt when they fail to live up to cultural demands and role expectations. This helps to explain how men and women enact their husband and wife roles. For example, many married women—in order to live up their ideal image of a "good wife"—are willing to defer to their husbands' migration decisions.

• Four common stances taken by marriage partners when problems arise are the super-reasonable, the irrelevant, the placater, and the blamer. The super-reasonable stance is one in which a partner uses intellect and reason and ignores the feelings of the other. The irrelevant stance is one in which partners change the subject to an unrelated topic when they become uncomfortable. The placater stance is one in which a partner seeks peace at any price and takes a "Whatever you want is fine with me" attitude. The blamer stance is one in which a partner accuses the other when things go wrong, rather than discuss the issue. All of these stances are fairly ritualized and tend to prevent closeness and intimacy from developing.

• Chemically dependent marital partners often use a pattern of shifting stances known as the "Karpman drama triangle," in which they rotate between victim, persecutor, and rescuer. The persecutor tends to elicits a victim response in the partner, and the victim position tends to pull the partner into the rescuer position. This pattern is not confined to chemically dependent partners, but can develop with any marital problem that goes unsolved.

• Marital satisfaction tends to be high for newly married couples, decrease during the childbearing and childrearing years, and increase during the "empty nest" stage. Young marrieds often experience a life cycle squeeze—problems surrounding the simultaneous launching of a family and a career. During this time a wife may have her lowest level of power in a relationship when she is raising children and unemployed. Additional stress occurs as the husband devotes a great deal of time to his career.

•A decline in marital satisfaction generally occurs during the early years of marriage whether or not the couple has children. However, the arrival of children does tend to decrease satisfaction with regard to the division of household labor and companionship. Further, there are differences in the ways in which husbands and wives react to the arrival of children. Husbands tend to experience the most difficulties in marital adjustment immediately following the birth of the first child and find greater satisfaction when the children enter their toddler years. Wives tend to face more difficulty and stress when the children become preschoolers.

Husbands who are late childbearers (age 28 or older) tend to be more egalitarian with regard to household labor, child care, and attitudes toward their wives. Wives who are late childbearers (age 25 or older) experience a role hiatus in which she takes a break between the daughter and mother roles and has time for employment before becoming a parent. Both of these late childbearing trends tend to promote marital stability.

• During the "empty nest" stage, the couple begins to focus attention more on couple activities and concerns and personal development. This may create anxiety at first. Husbands tend to appreciate the new focus whereas wives find it difficult to adjust to the waning of the parental role.

• Women are more likely than men to fall into the caregiving role when they are elderly. Caregiver wives tend to have lower levels of well-being, more poor health and depression, and more marital difficulties than other wives. Since women typically play the caregiving role in marriage, men whose wives die suddenly often find it difficult to adjust.

• Although same-sex marriages are not legal, same-sex partnerships are beginning to gain some legal rights. Some major cities have passed domestic partners legislation which enables the same-sex domestic partners of city employees to enjoy some of the benefits usually available to married spouses.

• Same-sex partnerships offer some freedom to the partners to move out of the restrictions imposed by traditional gender roles. Same-sex relationships tend to be more androgynous with regard to household chores than heterosexual partnerships. Same-sex partnerships tend to stress equality more than heterosexual relationships.

• Lesbian women usually have more committed partnerships than gay men. For lesbian women, commitment usually includes sexual exclusivity. Gay men often view commitment and sexual exclusivity as separate issues. Jealousy is less socially acceptable among gay men than among heterosexuals. Like heterosexuals, gay men manage their emotions so as to bring them into conformity with the social expectations of their community.

• Relationships with kin are often a source of strain for both gay men and lesbian women. Although it is a source or tension for both, lesbians are less likely than gay men to reveal their sexual orientation to relatives or friends. As a result of their greater secrecy, lesbians are often less integrated into a supportive homosexual community than gay men.

NOTES:

KEY TERMS

The following key terms are found in your textbook on the page number indicated in parentheses. In the space provided, write a brief definition of the key term. Then provide an example of the term, such as a culture in which the practice takes place, or people that you might know whose behavior illustrates the term. You could include issues that you might have read about in the news or in a book, or anything else that will illustrate the term and help you remember it. Include any comments from your class discussions or textbook that might help you remember and understand these key terms.

marital quality (satisfaction) (p. 175)

____

____

____

marital stability (p. 175)

____

____

____

marital success (p. 175)

____

____

____

family ritual (p. 175)

____

____

cross-complaining (p. 176)

self revelation (p. 176)

intimacy (p. 178)

commitment (p. 178)

selection hypothesis (p. 180)

protection hypothesis (p. 180)

happiness gap (p. 182)

ideal self (p. 184)

tyranny of the shoulds (p. 184)

marital stances (p. 186)

super-reasonable stance (p. 187)

irrelevant stance (p. 187)

placater stance (p. 187)

blamer stance (p. 187)

Karpman drama triangle (p. 187)

victim stance (p. 187)

persecutor stance (p. 187)

rescuer stance (p. 187)

life cycle squeeze (p. 188)

role hiatus (p. 191)

domestic partners (p. 193)

domestic partner legislation (p. 194)

androgyny (p. 194)

NOTES:

PRACTICE TEST

Multiple Choice

1. Social scientists have found that marital quality:
   a) is more or less predetermined by patterns that are set by the time a couple decides to get married
   b) is relatively unaffected by the quantity and quality of rituals engaged in by the family
   c) increases with moderate levels of self-revelation between the spouses but decreases with too little or too much self-revelation
   d) increases continuously as self-revelation between the spouses increases

2. The dying American ritual of having a sit-down family dinner:
   a) tends to increase marital quality because it promotes independence among all family members
   b) tends to increase marital quality because it enables the spouses to spend time away from each other
   c) tends to decrease marital quality
   d) has had no detectable effect on marital quality

3. Marital quality is more likely to increase when:
   a) couples avoid cross-complaining
   b) spouses are direct in pointing out what bothers them about each other's personality rather than by talking about issues
   c) spouses speak their mind immediately when something bothers them
   d) spouss are open and critical with each other rather than censoring their thoughts

4. In a marriage relationship, as in other relationships where there are differences in power among the people involved:
   a) high self-revelation on the part of the subordinate partner is likely to increase his or her power
   b) low self-revelation on the part of the subordinate partner is likely to increase his or her power
   c) low self-revelation on the part of the subordinate further increases the power of the dominant partner
   d) there is very little that can be done to change the balance of power once it has become established

5. The protection hypothesis holds that:
   a) people who have emotional or physical problems are probably considered less desirable marriage partners than healthier people
   b) the continuous companionships, emotional support, and interpersonal closeness provided by marriage acts as a buffer against the stress of daily living
   c) married women tend to be happier if their husbands fulfill the traditional instrumental gender role of provider
   d) couples who fulfill traditional gender roles are less affected by changes in social institutions such as religion, the economy, and government

6. From the early 1970s to the late 1980s the happiness gap between married people and single people:
   a) has remained about the same for both women and men
   b) has decreased for women, but increased for men
   c) has increased for women, but decreased for men
   d) has decreased for both women and men

7. Karen Horney argues that the "tyranny of the 'shoulds'" results <u>from</u>:
   a) broad self-revelation
   b) lack of empathy
   c) an image of an ideal self
   d) husband-centered migration patterns

8. A study sponsored by the Canadian government found that the factor of greatest importance in explaining the willingness of wives to defer to their husband's decision to move was:
   a) the educational level of wives
   b) the occupational status of wives
   c) the occupational and educational level of husbands
   d) traditional gender roles

9. The Canadian government survey mentioned above also found that well-educated employed wives and wives whose education or occupational status was superior to that of their husbands:
   a) were much less likely to defer to their husbands' decisions to move because they had the resources to enable them to resist
   b) were more likely to defer to their husbands' decisions to move because they knew they would have an easier time becoming re-employed
   c) were just as likely as less educated wives to follow their husbands' decisions
   d) were much more likely to initiate a divorce than less educated wives with lower occupational status

10. Marital stances in which marital roles are enacted:
a) are more likely to occur when marital partners fulfill traditional gender roles
b) are more likely to develop when marital partners do not fulfill traditional gender roles
c) often arise in stressful situations and generally help to create marital stability
d) often arise in stressful situations and tend to perpetuate marital distress

11. Four common marital stances in which marital roles are enacted are:
a) super-reasonable, irrelevant, placater, and blamer
b) super-reasonable, unyielding, unreasonable, and blamer
c) vertical, horizontal, super-reasonable, and placater
d) vertical, super-reasonable, placater, and traditional

12. In the super-reasonable stance, one partner:
a) uses intellect and reason but ignores the feelings of the other
b) uses intellect and reason and considers the feelings of the other
c) tries to make sure that the other partner has an equal chance of winning an argument
d) insists that each partner's position is equally viable and is primarily concerned with the welfare of the marriage

13. The pattern of shifting stances between victim, persecutor, and rescuer often used by chemically dependent partners is known as:
a) Carpe diem
b) Karposi's sarcoma
c) Karpman drama triangle
d) the reverse blame syndrome

14, Marital satisfaction tends to:
a) increase steadily over the life cycle
b) decrease somewhat during the child-rearing years, and rise again during the "empty nest stage"
c) increase during the child-rearing years and decrease during the "empty nest" stage
d) decrease steadily over the life cycle

15. Which of the following is NOT usually an explanation for changes in marital satisfaction following the birth of a child:
a) the life cycle squeeze
b) changes in marital power
c) husband's career commitment
d) changes in physical appearance

16. With regard to childbearing and childrearing, wives report that they have the most difficulties coping:
   a) immediately following the birth of the first child
   b) when children enter the preschool years
   c) during the teen years
   d) during the "empty nest" stage

17. Husbands who become fathers at a later age tend to:
   a) be more egalitarian with regard to household labor and childrearing than husbands who have children earlier
   b) more traditional in their attitudes and practices of household labor and childrearing than husbands who have children earlier
   c) be less tolerant of the wife during childrearing years than husbands who have children earlier
   d) less educated than husbands who have children earlier

18. Same-sex relationships tend to:
   a) be much more rigid in their enactment of traditional gender roles than heterosexual relationships
   b) be more likely to involve androgynous gender roles than heterosexual relationships
   c) exhibit more satisfaction if their is a clear dominant-subordinate relationship between the partners
   d) have more tension when equality between the partners exists

19. Lesbian women usually:
   a) have more committed partnerships than gay men
   b) have less committed partnerships than gay men
   c) make a distinction between commitment and sexual exclusivity
   d) are more integrated into the homosexual community than gay men

20. Among gay men, jealousy:
   a) is considered to be an emotion that one is born with and, therefore, widely tolerated
   b) occurs much more often than among heterosexuals
   c) never occurs
   d) is considered less socially acceptable than among heterosexuals

NOTES:

PROJECTS

PROJECT 7. 1 Marital Quality in Your Family

As you have read in Chapter 7 of your textbook, marital success refers to a marriage which both lasts **and** has a high level of marital quality or satisfaction. The quality of a marriage, and, hence the amount of happiness people derive from their marriage, has been found to be associated with a number of factors including family ritual, spending time together, positive communication patterns, self-revelation, intimacy, commitment, and religious belief. The objective of this project is to have you gain insight into what contributes to a successful and happy marriage.

Journal instructions:

1. Re-read the section in chapter 7 that deals with marital quality. In the space provided on the next page, summarize each of the factors that have been associated with marital quality and provide an example.

2. Each day for one week, use the spaces provided on the following pages to observe and reflect upon marital quality in your family now and/or when you were growing up. If you are living at home, base your journal primarily on your observations of activities that occur during the week. What family rituals took place? Were there any positive communication patterns that took place? How was intimacy or commitment demonstrated? Were religious beliefs demonstrated in any way? Be sure to look very carefully and with a keen eye. If you are not living at home, use the week's time to reflect on activities that are related to marital quality when you were living at home. Provide explicit examples and be as thorough as possible. If you do not observe a particular factor, or do not recollect one, explain why you think it did not occur. If you have trouble recollecting things, feel free to use your parents as consultants for this activity. If you use up the space provided on any one day, use additional paper.

Option: essay

Write an essay (around five pages, typed) in which you use the observations and reflections you compiled on the following pages, and the material found in the section on marital quality in Chapter 7 in your textbook, to discuss marital quality in **your** family now and when you were growing up.

Option: bibiography

Develop a bibliography that includes five to ten articles from social science journals and five to ten articles from popular periodicals about marital quality or factors related to marital quality. As you search through the indexes in the library you might consider using marital quality or any of the factors related to marital quality as key words to conduct your library search. Type your bibliography using the format found in your textbook or in the journal articles.

Option: research paper
Use material from at least five items in your bibliography and data that you collected about your family (above) to write a paper (around seven to nine pages, typed) in which you discuss factors related to marital quality. Make sure that at least two of the articles that you use are from social science journals. Be sure to provide proper documention throughout your paper and provide a reference (works cited) page.

DEFINITIONS AND EXAMPLES: Fill in the spaces below with definitions and examples of the following factors that are related to marital quality.

Family ritual

Spending time together

Positive communication patterns

issues versus personality

avoiding cross-complaining

Self-revelation

Intimacy

Commitment

Religious beliefs

Day 1
Family ritual

Spending time together

Positive communication patterns

issues versus personality

avoiding cross-complaining

Self-revelation

Intimacy

Commitment

Religious beliefs

Day 2
Family ritual

Spending time together

Positive communication patterns

issues versus personality

avoiding cross-complaining

Self-revelation

Intimacy

Commitment

Religious beliefs

Day 3
Family ritual

Spending time together

Positive communication patterns

issues versus personality

avoiding cross-complaining

Self-revelation

Intimacy

Commitment

Religious beliefs

Day 4
Family ritual

Spending time together

Positive communication patterns

issues versus personality

avoiding cross-complaining

Self-revelation

Intimacy

Commitment

Religious beliefs

Day 5
Family ritual

Spending time together

Positive communication patterns

issues versus personality

avoiding cross-complaining

Self-revelation

Intimacy

Commitment

Religious beliefs

Day 6
Family ritual

Spending time together

Positive communication patterns

issues versus personality

avoiding cross-complaining

Self-revelation

Intimacy

Commitment

Religious beliefs

Day 7
Family ritual

Spending time together

Positive communication patterns

issues versus personality

avoiding cross-complaining

Self-revelation

Intimacy

Commitment

Religious beliefs

PROJECT 7. 2 Stances in Marriage and Intimate Personal Relationships

As Wolf notes in chapter 7, marriage partners often develop familiar ways—or stances—to enact their marital roles: the super-reasonable, the irrelevant, the placater, and the blamer stances. These stances often arise in stressful situations and tend to perpetuate marital distress. Do we also enact these stances outside of marriage in other intimate relationships? The objective of this activity is to help you understand how easy it is to adopt these stances and how they can perpetuate distress in marriage and other intimate personal relationships.

Journal instructions:

1. Re-read the section in Chapter 7 that discusses marital stances and marital distress. In your journal, summarize each of these stances and provide an example.

2. For one to two weeks, observe instances of the four stances that take place in your family, among friends, in your personal relationships, in movies, and in television programs. Do not restrict your observations only to marital relationships but focus on any intimate personal relationships that might exhibit stances that people use in stressful situations. If you wish, you may choose to focus exclusively on one relationship. You do not necessarily have to be involved in the relationship you are observing. In your journal, record each instance in detail and explain which marital stance it illustrates.

3. After each observation of a stance that you make, also discuss what the reaction of the other person was and what its effect was on the stressful situation. Did it help the relationship? Did it hinder it? Did it make no difference?

Option: essay

Write an essay (around four to five pages, typed) in which you use your observations and the material on marital stances in Chapter 7 to discuss how the marital stances that Wolf discusses have been observed in intimate interpersonal relationships in the world around you. Be sure to address the question of whether or not these stances—or similar ones—are taken in relationships other than marital ones. You may focus on one particular relationship, or you may focus on intimate relationships in general.

NOTES:

CHAPTER 8

MARRIAGE, WORK, AND POWER

CHAPTER OUTLINE

Husbands, Wives, and Work
- Employment Over the Life Cycle

Working Wives Among Mexican-American Immigrant Families
- Economic Goals

The African-American Two-Earner Family
- African-American Men

Rewards and Costs of a Wife's Employment
- Rewards
- Costs

Household Labor
- How is Household Labor Divided?
- Ferree's Topology of Two-Earner Marriages
- Changing Family Roles
- Household Labor versus Total Labor
- The Problem with Counting Hours
- Responsibility for Child Care
- Perception of Fairness
- Perceptions that Promote Equity

Work-Family Conflict
- Negative Mood Spillover
- Role Overload
- Role Conflict

Strategies for Reducing Work-Family Conflict
- Role Reduction
- Lowering Standards for Role Performance
- Negotiating Reassignment of Role Duties
- Changing Work Conditions
- Social Redfefinition

Dual-Career Marriages
- Commuter Marriages
- Pressure for the Wife to Continue Working
- Couples with Equal Status of Occupations

Theories of Work and Power
- Conflict Theory
- Exchange Theory
- Gender Role Theory

CHAPTER LEARNING OBJECTIVES

After studying this chapter, you should be able to:

- discuss trends in labor force participation among married women and women in American society from the seventeenth century through the present;
- discuss the economic role of wives in Mexican-American immigrant families;
- discuss the challenges in combining work and family for African-American families;
- discuss the rewards and costs of a wife's employment;
- discuss the different ways in which the division of household labor has been depicted by social scientists;
- identify and discuss the strategies that employed wives use to arrive at a perception of fairness in the division of household labor;
- identify and discuss the three sources of work-family conflict;
- identify and discuss five strategies for reducing work-family conflict;
- discuss dual-career marriages as a special form of two-earner marriages;
- discuss the difference between power as influence and power as authority;
- identify and discuss three theories that attempt to explain power in relationships.

KEY POINTS FOR REVIEW

• In colonial American families of the seventeenth and eighteenth centuries, when the home and workplace were combined, both husbands and wives worked on the farm producing crops, clothing, and other items. When the United States became industrialized in the nineteenth century, most economic production moved outside the home and the husband-breadwinner, wife-homemaker family became the norm.

• Women's participation in the labor force increased dramatically during World War II, declined briefly after the war, had returned to the wartime level by 1947, and has continued to increase since then. Married women's participation in the labor force has nearly doubled since 1960. Today, only one in five families is a traditional family with a husband-breadwinner and a wife-homemaker.

• Most women (70 percent) are in the labor force by their early twenties and over 75% spend their midlife years in employment. Ninety-four percent of males are employed by their late twenties and tend to remain there until retirement. Historically, African-American wives have been more likely than white wives to be employed, but now both tend to remain in the labor force when they have children. Fifty-eight percent of all married women in the United States with a child under six are in the labor force.

• Wives in Mexican-American immigrant families that seek paid employment often face resistance stemming from traditional Mexican-American values of familism and patriarchy. Despite this resistance and their lack of language proficiency, education and job skills necessary for well-paid employment, the wife's income is frequently essential for the family to achieve a higher standard of living. To convince their husband that her employment is beneficial to the family, the Mexican-American wife often needs to convince her husband that the goals of basic subsistence, economic betterment, and economic security could be achieved only with her earnings.

• African-American married women are more likely to be employed than unmarried African-American women. African-American men tend to be more approving of a wife's employment than white men or Mexican-American men. Employed African-American wives report being less satisfied with family life than African-American wives who are not employed. Being a good provider to the family and achieving steady employment are central to the self-image of African-American middle-class men. African-American men with irregular employment who do most of the household chores tend to be less satisfied with life than African-American men who do less household work.

• The economic advantage of wives' employment varies with the husbands' earnings. The economic benefits of a wife's employment is greatest in low-income families. Once a wife in a low-income family becomes a mother, the economic benefits of her employment decrease. As the husband's income rises, the relative economic benefit of the wife's employment decreases. The costs of the wife's employment include work-related costs such as child care, meals eaten away from home, transportation, clothing and personal care, union dues, laundry service, social security, and other taxes. Nevertheless, the leftover income from a wife's earnings may be enough to sufficiently raise the family's standard of living.

• Ferree arrived at a topology of how household chores are divided in two-earner marriages. One-third included "drudge wives"—wives who work full time and perform more than 60 percent of household tasks. One-fourth included "semi-housewives"—wives who work part-time and perform 67 percent of the household tasks. One-third included "two-housekeeper couples," where husbands perform 40 percent or more of the household chores. Nine percent included "cash-paying couples" that purchased domestic services. Since the 1970s, the proportion of "drudge wives" has remained the same and the percentage of "two-housekeeper couples" has increased four-fold. Still, only around one-third of two-earner marriages approaches an equal division of household labor.

• While social scientists agree that wives do the majority of household chores, they disagree over the amount of inequity that actually exists in the division of household labor. Some social scientists argue that when the number of hours of total labor—that is, both paid employment and household labor, rather than only housework and child care—are examined, far less inequality exists in the marital division of labor. By contrast, other social scientists argue that counting the hours of housework produces an underestimate of the wife's contribution to the family. Besides actual time spent performing tasks, wives also spend time being responsible for the household and for childcare. There is a difference between parental responsibility, which wives are generally accountable for, and parental assistance.

• Even though wives generally do more housework than husbands—regardless of the definition of household labor that is used—wives typically report that they consider the division of household labor to be fair. Wives use a number of strategies to arrive at a perception of fairness in the division of household labor including comparing their own time spent in housework to that of other wives, comparing their husbands' housework performance to that of other husbands, labeling many of their tasks as non-work, and rationalizing the husband's small contribution to household labor by thinking that he is incapable of doing a good job.

• Stress in families is often the result of trying to balance work and family life. In negative mood spillover, the problems and stress at work spill over and affect a person's ability to perform family roles. Role overload occurs when there is not enough time and energy and time available to perform requirements of one's roles—such as when an employed person finds that there is not enough time in the day to adequately fill all the demands of the parent role. Role conflict occurs when the requirements of two or more roles one plays are incompatible—such as when a parent has an important business meeting that cannot be missed and has a child at home sick with the flu. Each of these work-family conflicts has a negative affect on the quality of marriage.

• There are a number of strategies that couples use to attempt to reduce work-family conflict. First, couples may try to reduce responsibilities in their major roles. Wives often reduce their responsibilities by seeking employment in a female-dominated occupation whereas husbands are likely to reduce the number of hours they work. Second, people may lower the standards of a role performance, such as not having an impeccably clean house. Third, couples may reassign their respective role duties. Fourth, some people have the option of taking advantage of various changing work conditions that help reduce work-family conflict—such as flexible work schedules, telecommuting, and job sharing. Finally, if all else fails, couples may use social redefinition—for example, highlighting the advantages of dual-earner families—to reduce their work-family conflict.

• Dual-career marriages are special category of two-earner marriages. They usually pay higher salaries, require more education, and provide more opportunities for advancement and personal development than jobs that are not considered a career. While most dual-career marriages involve living at a common residence, some couples develop commuter marriages. Since careers often require that people keep up with new developments in their field in order for them to be promoted and advance, both partners often resume work soon after the birth of a child. Couples in occupations with equal status face additional strains since there is far less time available for either spouse to do domestic chores.

• There are two types of power: power as influence (using power to influence someone) and power as autonomy (using power to resist someone's influence). Three theories that attempt to explain power in relationships are conflict theory, exchange theory, and gender role theory.

• Conflict theory argues that the partner with the most resources in a marital relationship holds the greatest power. Resources include income, educational attainment, and occupational status. Some social scientists feel that personal resources—such as love, sex, companionship, affection, attention, intellectual stimulation, approval, emotional support, and personal services—are also a source or power. Conflict theory maintains that the dominant partner seeks to maintain the status quo by resisting attempts by the subordinate partner to bring about change. The division of household labor is frequently used as an indicator of power in marriage.

• Exchange theory argues that marriage is a relationship in which bargains are continuously negotiated and resources are constantly exchanged. This theory holds that partners weight the benefits and costs of a relationship and tend to remain in a relationship when the benefits outweigh the costs.

• Gender role theory argues that power in a relationship is established through socialization into traditional gender roles during childhood. Husbands are still expected to be the primary breadwinners and wives are still expected to have primary responsibility for the family household. Marriage partners can influence a spouse's behavior by appealing to gender role expectations.

KEY TERMS

The following key terms are found in your textbook on the page number indicated in parentheses. In the space provided, write a brief definition of the key term. Then provide an example of the term, such as a culture in which the practice takes place, or people that you might know whose behavior illustrates the term. You could include issues that you might have read about in the news or in a book, or anything else that will illustrate the term and help you remember it. Include any comments from your class discussions or textbook that might help you remember and understand these key terms.

labor force (p. 202)

____

____

____

leftover income (p. 209)

____

____

____

familism (p. 205)

____

____

____

patriarchy (p. 206)

____

____

household labor (p. 209)

drudge wife (p. 210)

two-housekeeper couple (p. 211)

total labor (p. 211)

parental responsibility (p. 212)

parental assistance (p. 212)

work-family conflict (p. 213)

negative mood spillover (p. 213)

burden-of-care explanation (p. 215)

role overload (p. 215)

role conflict (p. 215)

role reduction (p. 216)

humanistic perspective (p. 214)

gynocentric perspective (p. 214)

backlash (p. 214)

telecommuting (p. 218)

social redefinition (p. 218)

family leave policy (p. 218)

dual-career marriage (p. 220)

commuter marriage (p. 219)

power as influence (p. 220)

power as autonomy (p. 220)

conflict theory (p. 220)

economic resources (p. 221)

personal resources (p. 221)

exchange theory (p. 221)

alternative resources (p. 222)

family economy (p. 222)

gender role theory (p. 223)

NOTES:

PRACTICE TEST

Multiple Choice

1. The husband-breadwinner, wife-homemaker family:
    a) has always been the norm in American families
    b) became the norm for American families during the nineteenth century
    c) became the norm for American families during World War II
    d) is a universal family norm

2. The percentage of "traditional" American families today with a husband-breadwinner and a wife-homemaker is:
    a) 75%
    b) 50%
    c) 20%
    d) 10%

3. The percentage of all married women in the United States who are in the labor force with a child under age six is:
    a) 92%
    b) 75%
    c) 58%
    d) 36%

4. The resistance that Mexican-American immigrant husbands put up when their wives try to seek paid employment stem from traditional Mexican-American values related to:
    a) familism and patriarchy
    b) individualism and matriarchy
    c) individualism and patriarchy
    d) monogamy and matriarchy

5. The goals that Mexican-American immigrant wives often try to convince their husbands to accept so that they will allow them to enter the work force include all of the following except:
    a) basic subsistence
    b) economic betterment
    c) economic security
    d) spousal equality

6. African-American families with reversed traditional marital roles:
   a) tend to experience the same marital strain that occurs in white families
   b) tend to experience significantly more marital strain than in white families
   c) tend to experience significantly less marital strain than in white families
   d) tend to experience greater satisfaction than in white families

7. The economic benefits of a wife's employment are greatest in:
   a) upper income families
   b) middle income families
   c) lower income families
   d) lower income families with children

8. In her topology of two-earner families, Ferree argues that:
   a) the degree of inequality in household labor has not changed over the last three decades, even though there are more women in the workplace
   b) the degree of inequality in household labor has been exaggerated
   c) men now perform as many household chores as do women
   d) marriages in which wives do most of the household chores have virtually disappeared

9. According to Ferree's topology of two-earner families, the biggest change in the division of household labor that has occurred sine the 1970s is:
   a) the percentage of families with a "drudge wife" has significantly decreased
   b) the percentage of "two-housekeeper couples" has increased four-fold
   c) the percentage of "two-housekeeper couples" has decreased slightly
   d) families with "semi-housewives" have all but disappeared

10. When paid employment and household labor are used to measure equality in the division of household labor:
    a) husbands generally do more housework than wives
    b) husbands and wives do about the same amount of housework
    c) wives still generally do more housework than husbands
    d) there is no difference in the division of household labor regardless of the definition of household labor that is used

11. Which of the following is NOT discussed by Wolf as a strategy that wives use to arrive at a perception of fairness in the division of household labor:
    a) comparing themselves and their husbands to other wives and husbands
    b) labeling their own housework as "non-work"
    c) assuming that men are basically different from women
    d) hiring part-time domestic help and childcare workers

12. Negative mood spillover usually refers to:
    a) feeling preoccupied, fatigued, and irritable at home as a result of problems and stress at work
    b) feeling stressed out at the end of the day as a result of responsibilities associated with child care
    c) the inability to perform one's work adequately as a result of the demands and stress associated with childcare
    d) being abrupt with one family member as a result of having conflict with another family member

13. A situation in which a parent feels it is important to be at work for an important meeting and also feels it is important to be at home to attend to a sick child is an example of:
    a) role overload
    b) negative mood spillover
    c) role conflict
    d) role reduction

14. When an employed parent comes home at the end of the day and feels overwhelmed at prospect of cooking dinner for a child, helping a child with homework, taking the child to purchase a present for a birthday party, and so on, is an example of:
    a) role overload
    b) negative mood spillover
    c) role conflict
    d) role reduction

15. The primary strategy which couples use to reduce work-family conflict is:
    a) lowering standards for role performance
    b) negotiating the reassignment of role duties
    c) role reduction
    d) social redefinition

16. When other strategies of reducing work-family conflict fail, couples are most likely to:
    a) change their work conditions
    b) lower their standards for role performance
    c) negotiate the reassignment of role duties
    d) use social redefinition to reduce their feelings of stress

17. The Family Leave Bill requires:
   a) that all firms provide employees twelve weeks per year of paid leave for family emergencies
   b) that firms with fifty or more employees provide employees twelve weeks per year of unpaid leave
   c) that firms with fifty or more employees provide women twelve weeks per year of paid maternity leave
   d) that all firms provide women twelve weeks per year of paid maternity leave

18. In marriages where couples have occupations with equal status:
   a) there tends to be less marital strain than in marriages where couples have occupations with unequal status
   b) there tends to be more marital strain than in marriages with couples who have occupations with unequal status
   c) husbands and wives tend to split domestic chores equally
   d) husbands tend to do most of the domestic chores

19. The type of power which refers to the ability of a person to resist the influence of another person is:
   a) power as autonomy
   b) power as influence
   c) coercive power
   d) legitimate power

20. Which of the following is frequently used as an indicator of power in marriage?
   a) the division of household labor
   b) educational attainment
   c) occupational attainment
   d) amount of time spent doing paid employment

NOTES:

PROJECTS

PROJECT 8. 1 Is Household Equality Between Men and Women Increasing?

Social scientists disagree as to the amount of equality in the division of household labor that exists between husbands and wives. The following are a few typical situations in which parents in almost every family with children often find themselves: a pediatrician's office, a dentist's office, a PTA meeting, a school bus stop, a drop-off and pick-up area outside an elementary or middle school for children whose parents drive them, a child-care center early in the morning when children are being dropped off and at pick-up time, a grocery store, a playground, an afternoon elementary school program, an afternoon or evening children's sporting event, and many others. The objective of this project is to have you compare your conclusions about the division of household labor with the findings of social scientists,

Journal instructions:

1. Observe six or seven of the above situations (or others that you can think of) for around thirty minutes to an hour each and note how many men and home many women are caring for their children, or performing household or childrearing duties. Record your observations in your journal.

2. Think about the types of duties and responsibilities that have to be fulfilled by husbands and wives, for example, buying the food, preparing meals, washing the dishes, earning income, paying bills, fixing things round the house, and many others. Make a list of these items in your journal. (Ask your parents for some suggestions as to what to include on this list.) Then compare the way in which these responsibilities are, have been, and will be met in three generations of your family. How will they likely be carried out in your family when you get married (or, if you are already married, how are they fulfilled now), the family you were raised in, and the family in which your parents were raised (that is, your grandparents). If possible, discuss this with your parents and grandparents. In your journal, discuss why the duties and responsibilities in these families are/were distributed between the males and females.

3. Ask your parents, grandparents, friends, and others who may be married to explain why the household responsibilities are divided the way they are in their homes and record their answers in your journal.

Option: essay

Using your journal observations, interviews, and information in Chapter 8 about household labor, write an essay (around five pages, typed) in which you discuss which household and child rearing responsibilities are being fulfilled by males and females, and whether or not these responsibilities are shifting. In addition, incorporate into your essay a discussion of the following: Do the women in the household you observed have a second shift? How does Ferree's' topology of two-earner marriages apply to what you observed? Is there a perception of fairness within the relationships you observed?

Option: bibliography
Using your library's periodical and book indexes, develop a bibliography of fifteen to twenty articles from social science journals and books written by social scientists about gender equality (or inequality) with regard to household labor. Type your bibliography in proper bibliographic form, using the reference page in the social science journals or your textbook as an example.

Option: research paper
Write a paper (around seven to nine pages) in which you integrate ideas and findings from five of the sources in your bibliography with the information you wrote about in your journal to discuss the division of household labor in the family. Use information such as statistics on current trends, theories about gender inequality or gender socialization, examples from your journal and so on in your paper. Be sure to document your references throughout the paper and include a reference (works cited) page.

PROJECT 8. 2 Work-Family Conflict

Much of the personal and family distress that we face in our lives is the result of trying to balance the demands of work and family roles. Wolf discusses three specific types of role-related distress that many of us face: negative mood spillover, role overload, and role conflict. Re-read what Wolf says about these in Chapter 8. In addition to these role-related problems is another one: role ambiguity. Role ambiguity occurs when the expectations of a role are not clear. Thus, we may not understand what is expected of us. For example, "I want to have a non-traditional relationship with my spouse, but I am not always sure how I am supposed to act." The objective of this project is to help you understand that many of the personal and family issues we face are the result of role-related distress and are not necessarily the result of personality clashes.

Journal instructions:

1. If you have not already done so, re-read the section in Chapter 8 of your textbook about work-family conflict. In your journal, summarize the types of role-related problems that may exist within families (including role ambiguity, as mentioned above).

2. For one week, keep a journal in which you record the problems, crises, and stress that you face (and that you observe others facing, especially family-related problems) that result from negative mood spillover, role overload, role conflict, and role ambiguity. Explain how each problem is related to a role.

3. For each problem that you observe, suggest a way that it can be solved or dealt with. You may use some of the strategies for reducing work-family conflict that Wolf suggests in Chapter 8, or you may think of some other strategies. **Be sure that your strategy is related to the fact that these are role-related problems.**

Option: essay

Write an essay (around four pages, typed) in which you discuss role-related problems that occur in people's personal lives. In your essay be sure to incorporate a summary of your observations, a discussion of your strategies, and material from the relevant sections in chapter 8 of your textbook.

Option: bibliography

Conduct library research to develop a bibliography of ten articles from social science journals that deal with issues related to role-related problems in families (negative mood spillover, role overload, role conflict, and role ambiguity). Type your bibliography in proper bibliographic form following the format found in the journal articles or in your textbook.

Option: research paper
Select two or more articles from your bibliography (above) that can provide you with insights about one or more of the problems you discussed in your journal or essay. Write a paper (around six to seven pages, typed) in which you use material from the journal articles to discuss the problems you selected from your journal or essay. Be sure to provide proper documentation throughout your paper and include a reference page.

NOTES:

CHAPTER 9

RACIAL AND CULTURAL DIVERSITY AMONG FAMILIES

CHAPTER OUTLINE

White Appalachian Families
- Relationship to the Land
- Family Size and Contraception
- Family Relationships
- Kin Networks
- Social Change

Hispanic-American Families
- Courtship and Marriage
- Machismo
- Teen Pregnancy and Marriage
- Children
- Women and Employment
- Social Change
- Familism

African-American Families
- Childrearing
- Employment
- Kin Networks
- Sources of Emotional Support
- African Heritage
- Current Migration Patterns
- Marriage Rate
- Misconceptions About the African-American Family

Fundamentalist Mormon Families Practicing Polygyny
- Historical Perspective
- Modern Polygyny
- Modern Mormon Families

Vietnamese-American Families

Downward Mobility

Gender Roles

Reconstructing Extended Families

Patriarchy and Women's Influence

Traditionalism

Vietnamese-American Parenting

CHAPTER LEARNING OBJECTIVES

After studying this chapter, you should be able to:

- discuss the distinct customs and culture of white Appalachian families that have developed as a result of their relative isolation in the valleys of the Appalachian mountains;
- identify and discuss family-related customs for Hispanic-Americans;
- discuss the ways in which the family has been a source of strength to African-Americans;
- discuss the misconceptions about the African-American family;
- discuss the historical development and practices of fundamentalist polygynous Mormon families;
- discuss family life of Vietnamese-American families especially with regard to changes resulting from downward mobility after migration and the loss of the extended family.

KEY POINTS FOR REVIEW

• Mountain Appalachian families usually settle in mountain valleys, called "hollers" and rely primarily on farming or mining for their livelihood. Most families own their own farm or rent land from relatives or from land companies. Coal mining has traditionally been the major source of employment, so when the use of coal as a fuel in the United States declined, widespread poverty occurred in Appalachia.

• Before children in Appalachian families inherit their parents' land, they must go through a trial period of many years in which they demonstrate their intention to settle down in the mountains.

Children who move away to the cities tend to become disinherited. In some cases, when the sons move away, the daughters may inherit the land. The eldest child does not necessary inherit the land. Often the youngest child inherits it, thus providing the parents with some security in their old age.

• In many isolated areas there are few convenient birth control services available. The typical household has six or more children. Public-health agencies have begun to establish family planning clinics in rural Appalachia which has led to a dramatic decline in family size in some areas. In areas where there are family-planning clinics, half of the women have opted for sterilization as a means of birth control.

• Appalachian culture exhibits male dominance. Men tend to control sexual encounters with their wives and determine the type of birth control to be used (which often is none). Women are expected to care for the family in the home and most mothers do not work at paid employment.

• Appalachian families have strong kin networks that they rely on for the exchange of services. Marriage frequently takes place within the larger kin group and it is not unusual to marry a close relative, such as a cousin.

• Striving for upward mobility is often viewed askance by mountain families. People who take advantage of educational opportunities are often said to be getting "above their raising."

• Courtship in Hispanic-American culture tends to be supervised by parents. Some young people elope to escape parental control. The young married couple typically moves in with the bride's parents—matrilocal residence. This helps provide the wife with influence in her family and enables the husband to escape the authority of his father. As the couple establishes their own home, the husband becomes the "jefe de la casa"—the boss of the house, yet his influence is never absolute.

• While machismo—male dominance in the family, pride in masculinity, and a belief in the double standard—is an important aspect of Hispanic-American culture, the degree of male dominance associated with machismo has been exaggerated. The wife has more honor and influence in the family than suggested by the stereotype of machismo. One positive aspect of machismo is that it helps to maintain the two-parent family system.

• In rural areas, when a teenage Hispanic-American girl becomes pregnant, both sets of parents force the couple to marry. Parental influence has diminished in urban areas. In the traditional Hispanic-American family, children are considered "the wealth of the poor." However, young marriage and childbirth tends to perpetuate poverty.

• Despite the Hispanic cultural ideal that disapproves of married women working outside the home, employment of married Hispanic women is increasing. Wives negotiate with their husbands and have to justify their employment in terms of improving the family's economic position. This is a source of much marital conflict in Hispanic-American families. Traditional Hispanic-American women feel more loyalty to support Hispanic culture than in joining the women's movement. Young educated Hispanic feminists, though, support women's rights.

• Familism—the idea that the welfare of the extended family is central and take priority over the needs of the individual—is an important value for Hispanic-Americans.

• The family has been a source of strength to African-Americans. Children are highly valued. The African-American family not only shelters its own children but often informally adopts the children of a relative or a friend. Parents provide the children with racial socialization, helping to prepare them for a life in a society which practices discrimination. The family also functions as a refuge for its members and helps them to cope with prejudice.

• African-American wives usually must be employed outside the home in order to help the family survive financially. Because of the dehumanized images of African-American males resulting from slavery, it is often easier for African-American women than men to obtain employment. Young African-American girls are socialized to expect to work at paid employment.

• The kin network serves as an important source of emotional and financial support in African-American families. In addition, a system of exchange of goods and services exists among many families in the form of helper networks. Friendships often consist of fictive kin—relationships that are modeled on family relationships. The strength of extended kin networks among African-Americans is rooted in African culture.

• During the early part of the twentieth century, African-Americans migrated to northern and western cities in search of factory employment. With the decline in factory work over the last fifteen years African-Americans have begun to return to the south.

• Most African-American women eventually marry, but almost one-third face a shortage of potential partners because of the high rate of joblessness, involvement with the criminal justice system, and high fatality rate among African-American men.

• Misconceptions about the African-American family have led to the assumption that it is disintegrating. Like other cultures, African-American families come in a variety of forms. The social problems approach to viewing the African-American family often overgeneralizes and frequently fails to take into account how African-Americans view their family experiences. African-American men play a larger role in the family than the stereotype portrays. African-American men and women tend to have the same values about marriage and the family as the larger culture, but often face greater obstacles.

• Although the Mormon church officially prohibits polygyny, there are around 50,000 people in polygynous marriages in the western United States, The founder of the Church of Jesus Christ of Latter Day Saints, Joseph Smith, and later his successor, Brigham Young, practiced polygyny and viewed it as an important part of religious practice. In 1887, Congress passed the Edmunds-Tucker Act which dissolved the Mormon church and confiscated its property. In response, the Mormon church and officially renounced polygyny. Nevertheless, a number of fundamentalist sects of Mormons continue to practice polygyny. Since the 1950s, "de facto" decriminalization of polygyny has been in existence. This means that in fact those who practice polygyny are not criminalized, even though "de jure" decriminalization of polygyny—that is, written laws decriminalizing polygyny—is not the case.

• Large families are desired among Mormons and an abundance of children is viewed as a sign of God's blessing. During the 1960s the birth rate in Utah was the highest in the industrialized world. The Mormon family is patriarchal with husbands having greater decision-making power than wives. In recent years, Mormon wives have begun to enter the labor force and the birth rate has declined. However, women are only allowed to work outside the home if the husband approves.

• Vietnamese families who arrived in the United States in the mid-1980s have had to cope with two major changes: downward mobility after immigration and the loss of the extended family as it had existed in Vietnam. In Vietnam, the cultural ideal dictated that a woman was to follow the authority of her father, then her husband, and then, when widowed, her eldest son. In reality, though, patriarchy was not as extensive as the cultural ideal would have it, and the wife was generally involved in family decision-making. The entry of Vietnamese-American women into the labor force in the United States has given them even more independence.

• When Vietnamese refugees entered the United States, they left many of the husband's kin behind in Vietnam which further increased the wife's influence in the family. With the loss of the extended families that they had in Vietnam, immigrants had to reconstruct new extended families with distant relatives and fictive kin. This led to the creation of large, complex households for Vietnamese-American families. The wives' influence is greater in these families than in traditional Vietnamese families. Nevertheless, Vietnamese-American women tend to retain their traditional values emphasizing patriarchy.

• As with many other immigrant families, familism is a strong value of the Vietnamese-American family. Another important value for Vietnamese-American families is filial piety, which refers to the child's respect, obligation, and obedience toward parents. This continues into adulthood and adult children are expected to support and care for their aging parents. Vietnamese-American parents are concerned that American culture and its emphasis on individualism may lead to an erosion of familism and filial piety.

KEY TERMS

The following key terms are found in your textbook on the page number indicated in parentheses. In the space provided, write a brief definition of the key term. Then provide an example of the term, such as a culture in which the practice takes place, or people that you might know whose behavior illustrates the term. You could include issues that you might have read about in the news or in a book, or anything else that will illustrate the term and help you remember it. Include any comments from your class discussions or textbook that might help you remember and understand these key terms.

hollers (p. 231)

____

____

____

mountain people (p. 231)

____

____

____

matrilocal residence (p. 233)

____

____

____

machismo (p. 234)

____

____

"jefe de la casa" (p. 234)

familism (p. 236)

racial socialization (p. 237)

fictive kin (p. 240)

polygyny (p. 242)

celestial marriage (p. 242)

de jure decriminalization of polygyny (p. 245)

de facto decriminalization of polygyny (p. 245)

family home night (p. 245)

downward mobility (p. 246)

reconstructing extended families (p. 247)

patrilocal residence (p. 247)

bargaining with patriarchy (p. 248)

asymmetrical bargaining (p. 248)

NOTES:

PRACTICE TEST

Multiple Choice

1. The people of the Appalachian mountains are primarily descendants of:
   a) German and Italian colonial settlers
   b) English and Scots-Irish colonial settlers
   c) Dutch and German colonial settlers
   d) Dutch and Swedish colonial settlers

2. Most Appalachian families:
   a) are landless
   b) rent their land
   c) own their own farm
   d) work in mills

3. When it comes to inheriting land in Appalachian families:
   a) the eldest child usually is first in line
   b) children must prove themselves worthy before they can inherit land
   c) children are provided land as an inducement not to move away
   d) women are virtually excluded

4. The major form of birth control for Appalachian women who attend family planning clinics is:
   a) the birth control pill
   b) the condom
   c) rhythm
   d) sterilization

5. Appalachian families settle in mountain valleys called:
   a) hollers
   b) yellers
   c) callers
   d) criers

6. People in Appalachian families that take advantage of educational opportunities usually:
   a) have higher prestige
   b) are usually called upon to be the community decision-makers
   c) are looked down upon
   d) return to their community to provide important services

7. After they get married, the young Hispanic-American couple usually practice:
   a) patrilocal residence
   b) matrilocal residence
   c) neolocal residence
   d) bilocal residence

8. The typical residential practice of the young Hispanic-American couples fulfills the following functions EXCEPT:
   a) it increases the wife's influence and status in the family
   b) it enables the husband to escape the authority of his father
   c) it strengthens the bride's relationship with her in-laws
   d) it strengthens the bride's relationship with her mother and sisters

9. The Hispanic-American cultural ideal of machismo:
   a) assures the husband complete domination over his family
   b) leads to a breakdown of the two-parent family
   c) does not provide the extent of male dominance that the stereotype suggests
   d) provides the wife with the ultimate decision-making power in the family

10. In rural areas, when a teenage Hispanic-American girl becomes pregnant:
   a) the girl's parents force the couple to marry
   b) the boy's parents force the couple to marry
   c) both sets of parents force the couple to marry
   d) the girl generally has an abortion

11. In the Hispanic-American culture, familism refers to:
   a) the practice of having the bride's family interview the groom's family before establishing a wedding date
   b) the practice of fasting on the night before the wedding
   c) the custom of having the new couple refrain from sexual intercourse until after a ritualistic meeting with their respective in-laws
   d) the value that places the welfare of the extended family above the needs of the individual

12. African-American wives and children:
   a) contribute a larger portion of family income than do white wives and children
   b) are much less likely to be employed than white wives and children
   c) rarely are employed outside of the home
   d) often rely on welfare employment only as a last resort

13. Young African-American girls are typically raised:
a) to expect to work outside the home
b) to be primarily ornamental
c) have low educational and occupational aspirations
d) to manipulate the welfare system

14. Fictive kin in African-American families are:
a) role models found in literature written by African-Americans
b) close relationships among non-relatives modeled after family relationships
c) people who pretend to be distant relatives in order to fulfill their own emotional and financial needs
d) much less likely to occur than among white families

15. The strength of the extended kin network among African Americans today has its roots in:
a) the period immediately after the Civil War when African-Americans began to migrate to the north
b) the Civil Rights Movement that took place in the 1960s
c) traditional African culture
d) the period in American history when African-Americans were slaves

16. Polygynous marriage among Mormons:
a) has virtually disappeared
b) officially is prohibited by the law and by the Mormon church, but still exists and generally is allowed to continue by those who enforce the law
c) is the official doctrine of the Mormon church, yet those who practice it usually face criminal charges
d) was never explicitly intended by the Mormon founder, Joseph Smith, nor his successor, Brigham Young

17. In Mormon families that practice polygyny:
a) the higher number of wives tends to increase the decision-making power of the women
b) women are encouraged to work outside the home in order to better provide for the family
c) there is less emphasis on the family as a social unit
d) the family is patriarchal with husbands having greater decision-making power than wives

18. In recent years, the birth rate in Mormon families in Utah:
a) has risen in comparison to the rest of the United States
b) has tended to remain about the same as it always has, in spite of changes in women's roles
c) has declined in comparison to the rest of the United States
d) has doubled since the 1960s

19. The "three obediences" that the Vietnamese woman was expected to follow under their patriarchal system included all of the following except obedience to her:
a) father
b) brother
c) husband
d) son

20. Traditional Vietnamese culture emphasizes filial piety, which refers to:
a) the child's respect, obligation, and obedience toward parents
b) the wife's submission to the demands of her husband
c) the husband's absolute allegiance to remaining faithful to the wife
d) the belief that since children are the future, their needs come before the parents' needs

NOTES:

PROJECTS

PROJECT 9. 1 Understanding Racial and Cultural Diversity Among Families

This project is similar to Project 1.3. As emphasized in Chapter 1, families in American society are becoming increasingly diverse, both structurally and culturally. Much of this diversity stems from racial and cultural differences of different groups in American society. Family economic systems, sexual practices, child rearing practices, husband-wife relationships, parent-child relationships, employment patterns, kin networks, family values and many other factors vary among the different racial and cultural groups, yet all co-exist within American society. It is important for us to understand that the "traditional" white middle class family is only one family type among many. The objective of this activity is to help you gain some important insights about the diversity that exists among American families and the reasons why the various forms exist.

Journal instructions:

1. Re-read Chapter 9. After you do so, look over the chapter outline located at the beginning of the chapter in the book or in this study guide. Under each family heading (for example, white Appalachian families, Hispanic-American families, and so on) you will see a number of items listed. In your journal, list each item (from all the family types) that you can comment on in relation to your family of orientation (the family in which you were raised) or your family of procreation (the family you created through marriage). Then, comment on how your family deals with that particular item. For example, under "relationship to the land," what can you say about your family's system of passing on property to family members? Under "family size and contraception," what can you say about norms regarding family size and contraceptive practices that affect your family? And so on. Obviously, there are some items that are not relevant to your family and you will not be able to comment on. Comment on as many as possible.

2. Identify a person you know whose family of orientation or family of procreation is racially, ethnically, or culturally different from yours. Try to select one of those discussed in Chapter 9, if possible. Discuss with the person you identified each of the items that you commented on in your journal and compare each of your families' practices with regard to them. Ask the person to explain why these practices make sense within his or her family. Write detailed notes of your discussion in your journal.

3. Spend four or five hours with the person you identified and his or her family. If this is not possible, try to have the person you identified spend a few hours with you and discuss, in detail, what life is like in his or her family. Afterwards, reflect and write about your views about this

person's family and the way that it operates and compare it with the views you held about this type of family before you learned about from your friend. Have your judgments about this type of family changed? Do the behaviors that you learned about make sense within the context of that family?

4. Identify four occupations in which knowledge of racial and cultural family diversity may be useful. List these in your journal and briefly discuss how/why this knowledge would be useful in these occupations.

Option: essay
Use your journal notes to write an essay (around three to five pages, typed) in which you compare your family with the type of family that you identified above.

Option: bibliography
Complete the above journal instructions. Then, through library research, compile a bibliography of ten to fifteen sociology articles and/or books (excluding textbooks) about the type of family that you learned about in your journal activity. For example, if the person you identified is from a Vietnamese-American family, then compile a bibliography of articles about Vietnamese-American families. Type your bibliography following the format used in your textbook or found in the sociology articles.

Option: research paper
If you have not already done so, complete the above journal and bibliography activities. Write a paper (around five to seven pages, typed) in which you use your journal and four or five articles from your bibliography to compare and discuss the values and practices in your family with the values and practices of the family you identified above. In your paper, include a discussion of why and how this knowledge is useful within different occupations. Provide proper documentation of your references throughout the paper and include a reference page.

NOTES:

CHAPTER 10

SOCIAL CLASS AND POVERTY

CHAPTER OUTLINE

The American Social Class Structure

The Lower Class: The Poor
- Fluidity
- The Working Poor
- Race, Ethnicity, and Poverty Rates
- Age
- The Feminization of Poverty
- The Underclass

Working Class
- The Organization of Work
- Working-Class Childrearing
- Marital Interaction
- Economic Insecurity
- Shrinking Opportunity Structure
- The African-American Family
- Health Insurance Coverage
- The Changing Organization of Work

Middle Class
- Home Ownership
- African-Americans in the Middle Class

Upper-Middle Class
- Separation from Lower Social Classes
- Job Insecurity in Middle- and Upper-Middle Class Families

Upper Class

The Homeless
- Who Are the Homeless?
- Homeless Individuals and Their Kin
- Explanations for Homelessness

CHAPTER LEARNING OBJECTIVES

After studying this chapter, you should be able to:

- identify and discuss the determinants of a family's social class position;
- identify and discuss the social forces that underlie poverty in American society;
- discuss the nature of working class employment;
- discuss the ways in which social class affects working-class family relationships such as child-rearing, marital interaction, and marital quality;
- discuss how economic conditions that have affected working-class families over the past three decades;
- discuss the impact of deindustrialization on the African-American family;
- discuss how the issue of health insurance coverage is particularly relevant to working-class families;
- discuss the income, occupational, and lifestyle characteristics of middle class families;
- discuss the income, occupational, and lifestyle characteristics of upper-middle class families;
- discuss how and why economic uncertainty affects middle- and upper-middle class families;
- describe the occupational and social activities of the upper-class families;
- discuss who the homeless are;
- explain why the kin of homeless men do not offer them housing;
- discuss the personal problems explanation and the structural conditions explanation of homelessness.

KEY POINTS FOR REVIEW

• The social class position of a family is determined by wealth (property owned), power (the ability to influence the lives of others), and prestige (admiration and respect). These determinants are typically indicated by income and occupation.

• Fourteen percent of Americans (37 million people) fall below the poverty line ($14,333 for a family of four). Further, there are a number of American low-income working-class families who are at risk of being drawn below the poverty line ("one recession, one illness, one accident away from being poor"). There is considerable movement in and out of poverty, especially for Hispanic- and African-Americans. More than half of poor heads of household work at least part of the year.

• Poverty rates are useful because they allow us to determine an individual's risk of being in poverty. African-Americans, Hispanic-Americans, Native Americans, children, and the elderly are the most likely to be poor. In addition, there is a growing trend toward the feminization of poverty—the tendency for poor families to be headed by single women.

• The most disadvantaged section of the poor that exists at the bottom of the social class ladder has been termed the underclass. The term "underclass" has been criticized as stigmatizing all the poor as consisting of families that have a single set of values that reject the ethic of honesty and hard work. The term "ghetto poor" has begun to be used as a more neutral term, but the term "underclass" is still widely used by the media and social scientists.

• The working class have blue-collar and pink-collar jobs which involve factory and construction work and low-skilled service work. These jobs typically offer hourly wages rather than annual salaries and provide low levels of economic security. The jobs tend to be repetitive and monotonous, and the workers have little sense of autonomy.

• Working-class parents tend to stress obedience and conformity when raising children. Since working-class jobs are usually not a source of gratification, but a means of earning a living, the family is looked to as the source of life satisfaction. Working class couples tend to marry early, usually soon after leaving high school. Blue-collar husbands experience more negative mood spillover from their jobs and express more complaints to their wives than white-collar husbands. Conversely, blue-collar wives tend to express fewer complaints than white-collar wives. Economic pressures often lead to marital tension and diminished marital satisfaction in working-class families. Working-class husbands tend to embrace traditional utilitarian gender roles associated with masculinity when dealing with marital problems.

• A number of structural factors have contributed to the economic insecurity of working-class families over the past three decades. A shift from an industrial economy—based on factory production—to a post-industrial economy—characterized by information processing and services—the growth of a global economy, the technological revolution, and a general shift from production to service-sector jobs has led to the elimination of many jobs and fewer opportunities for working-class people.

• Employment opportunities in the north during and after World War II led to the establishment of many African-American urban communities. Because of housing discrimination, African-Americans of all social classes lived in similar communities. As a result, middle-class African-American families provided support networks for working- and lower-class African-Americans. This helped create a mechanism for upward mobility for African-American families. During the 1960s, the loss of jobs due to increased deindustrialization and the exodus of middle-class African Americans from the inner city in search of housing opportunities eroded the support networks that earlier had helped inner city African-American families achieve upward mobility.

• Working-class families face a particular predicament when it comes to health insurance coverage. They are less likely than the middle class to be covered by health insurance, yet typically are not eligible for government entitlement programs.

• For working class people who are fortunate enough to find stable factory work, the nature of factory work is changing. Workers are now expected to become involved in quality circles in which workers meet to discuss how to organize the workplace and produce products more efficiently. This tends to create a more positive attitude for workers and could have a positive effect on marital interaction.

• The middle class includes those families who earn incomes just above and below the median family income, which is currently $36, 812 per year. Some of the defining characteristics of the middle class are home ownership, a college education for their children, and family vacations. However, not all middle-class families can afford to purchase a home. Home ownership is more likely for non-Hispanic white families than for African-Americans or Hispanic-Americans. African-American families tend to have a less economically secure position in the middle class than white families.

• Upper-middle class professional families have white-collar jobs that are based on "mental work" rather than physical labor, offer a salary rather than an hourly wage, and offer a career path with promotion opportunities. Their life style includes the ability to afford such things as psychotherapy, fitness training, summer camp for children, and cultural activities. Unlike those with inherited wealth, the professional upper-middle class must work for a living. The upper-middle class tends to live in a relatively economically segregated social world that consists of other members in their social class position. This includes the use of private services—such as private schools, private transportation, private clubs, and so on—rather than public services.

• Middle- and upper-middle class families have begun to experience economic insecurity as a result of U.S. corporations having to downsize to remain competitive. Some restructuring results in permanently lost jobs. People in management positions have to spend a long time finding re-employment and often at a lower pay with fewer benefits than the previous job.

• The upper class—those with substantially higher incomes than people in the upper-middle class—consists of the lower-upper and upper-upper class. Families in the lower-upper class, the "nouveau riche" (newly rich), have newly acquired wealth whereas families in the upper-upper class, the “old rich,” have inherited family wealth. Families in the upper-class tend to associate with other upper-class people and develop their networks through private schools and private clubs.

• The homeless population consists of families as well as individuals. Homeless cohabiting couples and mother-headed families have often been overlooked. Homeless mothers tend to rely on hidden housing and avoid homeless shelters because they fear losing their children to the foster care system. Once lost to the system, it is difficult for single mothers to get their children back.

• Many homeless single men have relatives that do not provide them with housing. Two explanations for this are the social isolation perspective and the affiliation perspective. The social isolation perspective holds that the kin of some homeless men withdraw their support after they become emotionally and economically drained from providing it for a lengthy period. The affiliation perspective maintains that many homeless men do obtain emotional and economic support from relatives from time to time, but since their relatives are also likely to be poor they cannot offer them permanent shelter.

• There are two broad explanations for homelessness: personal problems and structural conditions. The personal problems explanation holds that the homeless suffer from a variety of personal afflictions—such as depression, mental illness, drug addiction, and alcoholism—that makes it difficult for them to hold permanent jobs or housing. A criticism of this explanation is that these personal problems may be the result of, as well as the causes of, homelessness. The structural conditions explanation contends that there are forces within the larger society—such as a decline in the stock of low-cost housing, rising rents, deinstitutionalization of the mentally ill, and changes in the occupational structure—that lead to homelessness.

KEY TERMS

The following key terms are found in your textbook on the page number indicated in parentheses. In the space provided, write a brief definition of the key term. Then provide an example of the term, such as a culture in which the practice takes place, or people that you might know whose behavior illustrates the term. You could include issues that you might have read about in the news or in a book, or anything else that will illustrate the term and help you remember it. Include any comments from your class discussions or textbook that might help you remember and understand these key terms.

social class (p. 257)

____

____

____

lower class (p. 257)

____

____

____

underemployed (p. 258)

____

____

____

poverty rate (p. 259)

feminization of poverty (p. 261)

underclass (p. 262)

working class (p. 264)

blue-collar jobs (p. 264)

pink-collar jobs (p. 265)

autonomy (p. 265)

skidding (p. 268)

standard of living (p. 268)

upward mobility (p. 268)

family wage (p. 268)

deindustrialization (p. 268)

global economy (p. 268)

technological revolution (p. 268)

two-tier society (p. 269)

production jobs (p. 270)

service jobs (p. 270)

opportunity structure (p. 270)

quality circles (p. 272)

middle class (p. 273)

median net worth (p. 275)

restructuring (p. 277)

downsizing (p. 277)

upper class (p. 278)

hidden housing (p. 279)

Aid to Families with Dependent Children (AFDC) (p. 280)

doubling-up (p. 281)

personal problems (p. 282)

economic defeatism (p. 282)

structural conditions (p. 282)

gentrification (p. 283)

deinstitutionalization (p. 283)

industrial economy (p. 267)

post-industrial economy (p. 267)

PRACTICE TEST

Multiple Choice

1. According to social scientists, a family's social class position is based on:
   a) wealth, power, and prestige
   b) wealth, power, and education
   c) wealth, education, and political party
   d) wealth, political party, and religion

2. The social class position of college students is determined by:
   a) their parent's income and occupation
   b) their social standing in the college community
   c) their GPA
   d) the occupation that they are likely to enter immediately upon graduation

3. What percent of Americans are poor?
   a) .4 percent
   b) 4 percent
   c) 14 percent
   d) 34 percent

4. The income for a family of four that is defined as the poverty line is:
   a) $10,500
   b) $14,300
   c) $16,200
   d) $18,300

5. The term "the feminization of poverty" refers to:
   a) the growing tendency for wives to earn a greater income than their husbands
   b) the growing tendency for poor men to have to take jobs traditionally filled by women
   c) the growing tendency for dual-earner families to be poor
   d) the growing tendency for poor families to be headed by women

6. William Julius Wilson's term for the most disadvantaged poor, "the underclass," has been criticized because:
   a) people from poor families have the same opportunities as people in middle class families
   b) the group he defines as the underclass really does not exist
   c) the term is outdated
   d) the term tends to stigmatize all poor people as having a set of values that rejects honesty and hard work

7. In raising their children, working class parents who have jobs requiring compliance to authority tend to:
   a) stress obedience and conformity
   b) encourage their children to question and challenge authority
   c) be more lenient and less punitive in disciplining children
   d) encourage their children to seek satisfaction outside of the family

8. Husbands with blue collar jobs:
   a) are less likely to complain to their wives than husbands with white collar jobs
   b) express more negative feelings and complaints to their wives than white collar husbands
   c) are less likely to complain about their jobs than wives with blue collar jobs
   d) have fewer job-related problems than white collar husbands

9. In *Worlds of Pain*, Lillian Rubin found that when working-class husbands discuss problems with their wives they:
   a) tended to use reason in approaching marital problems and were likely to avoid taking feelings into consideration
   b) tended to be overemotional and unreasonable
   c) tended to balance their emotions with reason
   d) tended to be egalitarian in their discussions with their wives

10. Which of the following is not a factor associated with de-industrialization?
    a) the global economy
    b) the technological revolution
    c) the emergence of a two-tier society
    d) greater equality among the social classes

11. The issue of health insurance in America is particularly relevant to the working class because:
    a) due to the nature of their jobs they are more likely to get sick than either the lower class or the middle class
    b) most "working class" illnesses are not covered by standard health insurance
    c) working-class families are less likely to be covered by health insurance, yet they are not eligible for government entitlement programs
    d) their are fewer hospitals in working class neighborhoods

12. The introduction of quality circles in factory work has:
    a) led to greater inequality between workers and management
    b) insured that most employees in factories will be covered by health care insurance
    c) helped to blur the distinction between managers and workers
    d) led to an increase in pay for managers

13. The median annual family income in the United States is currently closest to:
a) $25,000
b) $36,500
c) $45,000
d) $53,500

14. Compared to African-Americans, the median net worth of white-Americans is:
a) ten times greater than that of African-Americans
b) five times greater than that of African-Americans
c) twice as great as that of African-Americans
d) about the same as that of African-Americans

15. Which of the following is not generally a characteristic of upper-middle class families:
a) their jobs are based on mental work rather than physical work
b) they are generally paid a salary rather than an hourly wage
c) most of their income is based on inheritance rather than earned
d) they usually are involved in careers with promotion opportunities

16. Generally, the "capital" through which the upper-middle class develops its wealth is:
a) knowledge and skill
b) inheritance
c) political affiliation
d) physical endurance

17. The socio-economic status of upper-middle class families:
a) is virtually assured from generation to generation once it has been achieved
b) is usually achieved at first by physical labor
c) can never be lost because of the social network developed by upper middle class people
d) must be renewed in each generation

18. Today, many U.S. corporations are restructuring, or reorganizing, to become more efficient. As a result, people in middle- and upper-middle class occupations:
a) face many more opportunities than before and thus face greater possibilities for upward mobility
b) face greater economic security than before since the increased efficiency of the corporation assures greater job stability
c) face economic insecurity because restructuring often leads to downsizing and the elimination of management positions
d) face a greater possibility of being laid-off in their job, but face increase opportunities to find higher-paying jobs with better benefits

19. The major difference between lower-upper class and upper-upper class families is found in:
    a) the occupations in which they are employed
    b) the length of time that the family has had its wealth
    c) the schools that their children attend
    d) the country clubs in which they are members

20. Homeless mothers tend to rely on hidden housing because:
    a) they fear losing their children to the foster care system
    b) they cannot collect welfare if they have a permanent address
    c) they are hiding from their husbands
    d) they do not want to be helped

21. The personal problems explanation of homelessness holds that:
    a) structural conditions that lead to homelessness create personal problems for people
    b) the homeless suffer from a variety of personal afflictions that make it difficult for them to hold down permanent jobs or maintain permanent housing
    c) depression, alcoholism, and mental illness are the results of homelessness
    d) government entitlement programs diminish people's incentive to find work and permanent housing

22. Structural conditions that lead to homelessness include all of the following except:
    a) a decline in the stock of low-cost housing
    b) declining enrollment in colleges
    c) deinstitutionalization of the mentally ill
    d) changes in the occupational structure

23. The process by which the middle class renovates dilapidated housing previously used by the poor is called:
    a) gentrification
    b) urbanization
    c) dilapidization
    d) deinstitutionalization

24. Which of the following public assistance programs is commonly referred to as "welfare"?
    a) Food Stamps
    b) Social Security
    c) Supplemental Security Insurance
    d) Aid to Families with Dependent Children (AFDC)

25. Estimates of the number of homeless people in the United States range from:

a) 10,000 to 100,000
b) 50,000 to 200,000
c) 500,000 to 1 million
d) 500,000 to 3 million

PROJECTS

PROJECT 10. 1 How Much Does it Cost to Live? Why Are Some Families Poor?

Many Americans believe that the poor are responsible for their own poverty and that people on welfare could find work if they really wanted to do so. While some people are responsible for their own poverty, a significant number of poor people work, but earn too little to bring them out of poverty. The U.S. Government defines the poverty level at $14,333 annually for a family of four. Besides being an indicator of the number of people who are officially poor in the United States, this figure is one of the measures used to determine if people are eligible for particular forms of government assistance. Is this an accurate figure? Does this figure reflect what it costs a family of four to live in today's society? Are people poor because they do not work hard enough? The objective of this activity is to have you explore answers to these questions and to examine how much it costs for a family to live.

Journal instructions:

1. Prepare a budget of expenses for a family of four to live in the city in which you currently reside. Proceed as follows:
   a) Make three columns on a sheet of paper in your journal or notebook.
   b) Label the first column"budget items." In this column, list all of the items that have to be paid for each month. These include, but are not limited to, the following: housing (rent or mortgage), utilities (gas, electric, water), telephone, medical care (office visits, drugs, insurance), food, clothing, transportation (car payments, insurance, gas, other transportation expenses), education, and so on. Think about this list carefully and include any other items that should be on the list. You may want to ask your parents or someone who pays their family's bill for suggestions of what to include on this list.
   c) Label the second column "minimum monthly expense." In this column, estimate for each item in the first column what you think the absolute minimum monthly expense for that item would be. That is, what is the bare minimum that you think a family of four could spend on that item.
   d) Label the third column "projected monthly expense." In this column, take a more realistic approach. Estimate the expense that you think a family of four of which you are a member is <u>likely</u> to incur each month.

2. Using your monthly budget estimates, calculate the total annual expense. (That is, add up each column and multiply by twelve.) Based upon your budget estimates, these figures indicate the net income, that is income after taxes are taken out, that a family of four needs to meet their minimum living expenses and your projected living expenses.

3. Considering these estimates, how appropriate is the government's figure for the poverty level?

4. How many full time, minimum wage jobs would it take to meet the needs of the budgets you estimated?

5. Based upon your budget, what would the minimum wage per hour have to be for one person to support a family of four? What would it have to be for two people to support a family of four?

6. In light of your findings, think about and discuss in your journal why people are poor. Are people poor, as many Americans believe, because they are not determined enough to work?

Option: essay

Re-read the sections in chapter 10 on how people in the lower and middle classes can become poor. Write an essay (around three to five pages, typed) in which you use your journal material and information found in chapter 10 to discuss why there are so many poor families in the United States.

PROJECT 10. 2 Life Chances of the Rich-and-Famous - and the Not-So-Rich-and-Famous

A family's social class position can greatly affect its members life chances—the opportunities one has to improve his or her income or lifestyle. The objective of this activity is to have you examine how social class position of a family affects its members' life chances.

Journal instructions:

1. Locate two or three introduction to sociology textbooks. If you do not have one, look in your college or local library, ask a sociology professor if you can borrow a few, or ask to borrow one from students who have taken introduction to sociology. Read the chapter in the introduction to sociology textbook on social stratification and pay particular attention to the sections that discuss the relationship between social class position and life chances. Most introductory sociology books discuss this.

2. Think about and list in your journal all of the ways in which peoples' social class positions can affect (positively or negatively) their life chances and opportunities (for example, housing, medical care, life expectancy, education, employment, mate selection, family stability, justice, and so on).

3. For each item in your list, write two or three sentences on how a family's social class position can affect a person's life chances. Then, discuss how your family's social class position has affected <u>your</u> life chances.

4. After you complete the above steps, identify and locate a neighborhood in your area in which people from an obviously different social class position live. For example, if your family is middle class, find a lower class or an upper class neighborhood. By yourself or with one of your classmates, observe each neighborhood for two or three hours on two separate days. (If possible, do your observation with someone who is from a different social class position than you. You will be able to share important insights with each other that you might not see if you were on your own). Keep a journal in which you record your observations about everyday life in the neighborhoods. The following is a list of some items you can focus on, but do not feel limited to this list:

   a) the types and conditions of the houses;
   b) the types and conditions of the automobiles;
   c) the condition of the schools, inside and out;
   d) the condition of the public parks;
   e) the condition of the roads;
   f) the types of stores, their condition, the types of products available, and the quality of the products;
   g) the hospitals and medical facilities;
   h) the amount of police protection or police surveillance.

5. After you complete your observations, discuss the impact of social class position on people's life chances and opportunities in both communities that you observed.

Option: essay
Read the chapters on socialization from one or two of the introduction to sociology textbooks that you located. Using information from those chapters (theories about socialization and other ideas) and examples from your journal observations (above), write an essay (around five pages, typed) in which you discuss how social class position affects a person's life chances, opportunities, and sense of self. If you wish, you can make your self the focus of this essay.

Option: bibliography
Using the library's indexes, construct a bibliography of fifteen to twenty articles (primarily from social science journals) and books about how social class position affects people's life chances and opportunities. Use key words, phrases, or ideas such as stratification, housing, educational attainment, family stability, life expectancy, and others in your search through the library's references, indexes, and other resources. Type your bibliography using the style found in the journals or in your textbook.

Option: research paper
Write a paper (around seven to ten pages, typed) in which you integrate your journal discussions (above) and at least four items from your bibliography to discuss how your family's position in the stratification system has affected your life chances, your socialization, and your sense of self. You can use the bibliographic material in a variety of ways. For example, use it to help you explain how various aspects of social class position have affected your life; or you might use examples from your life to illustrate some of the ideas found in your library research material. Be sure to cite all of your bibliographic references properly in your paper, and include a reference (works cited) page.

NOTES:

PROJECT 10. 3 How Health Care Policies Will Affect Families in Various Social Classes

As indicated in Chapter 10, different social classes experience different types of health-care coverage. The new health-care policies that eventually will be enacted will affect us differently, depending upon which social class our family is in. The objective of this activity is to help you become familiar with the various policies being considered and to examine how they might affect people in the different social classes.

Journal instructions:

1. Discuss with your parents, spouse, or other family members the percentage of your family's annual income that goes toward health-care insurance. (If your family does not have health-care insurance, what percentage of its annual income is generally spent on health care?) Think about and discuss in your journal how your family will adjust to increasing health-care costs.

2. Health-care reform is a major political, as well as social, issue. Many policies have been suggested by politicians from both political parties regarding how health care will be paid for and the organization of the health-care system itself. Look through current and past issues of newspapers, magazines, and journals (use your library's indexes to help you locate appropriate articles) to identify two policies that have been proposed to deal with the cost of health care in the United States recently. In your journal, briefly outline what each of these policies proposes.

3. For each policy, think about and discuss in your journal what the implications are for your family, for other families in your social class position, and for families in other social class positions.

4. Interview two physicians and two federal, state, or local politicians (one Republican and Democrat) about the policies you identified. Ask them what their views are about the advantages and disadvantages of each policy. Also, ask them what they would recommend to help deal with the high cost of health care in the United States.

Option: essay

Write an essay (around five pages, typed) in which you discuss the health-care policies you identified (above) and how each of the social classes might be affected if each were to be enacted. Use information that you collected from your journal (above).

Option: bibliography

Use your library's indexes to generate a bibliography of ten to fifteen articles from social science journals, newspapers, magazines, commentary magazines, and so on that discuss the advantages and/or disadvantages of the policies you identified (above). Type your bibliography in proper bibliographic format.

Option: research paper

Using the material you collected in your journal (above) and the bibliography you developed, write a paper (around seven pages, typed) in which you:

a) present each policy;

b) present the arguments for and against each policy, including a discussion of the implications for different social classes and for the health-care system in general;

c) formulate an opinion on which of the two policies should be enacted and use at least five sources from your bibliography to support your argument.

Be sure to cite your sources throughout your paper and include a reference page.

NOTES:

PROJECT 10. 4 Homelessness

There are a number of perspectives and explanations about homelessness, as you have read in Chapter 10. The objective of this activity is to help you gain some insights about why people are homeless and to help you overcome some of the myths about homelessness.

Journal instructions:

1. Interview five people who are not experts in understanding the nature of homelessness. For example, interview some of your friends, your parents, neighbors, and so on. Ask them the following questions and record their answers in your journal:
   a) Do you personally know anyone who is homeless, that is, who sleeps on the streets, in a homeless shelter, in a car, or somewhere else besides a home?
   b) Why do you think that most people who are homeless are so?
   c) What do you think are some typical characteristics of homeless people?
   d) Do you think that all people could find a place to live if they really wanted to?

2. Locate and read four or five articles, essays, or letters to the editor about homelessness that appeared in newspapers or news magazines during the past year. In your journal, summarize the views about homelessness portrayed in the articles, essays, or letters.

3. Visit a homeless shelter in your area. Observe it for one or two hours on three separate occasions and at different times of the day (morning, midday, and night). Talk to as many of the people there as you can. Ask them why they are there and what conditions led them to become homeless. Also, talk to the director of the homeless shelter. Ask the director if homelessness is increasing in the area and the reasons for the increase or decrease in homelessness. Record these discussions in your journal.

4. In your journal, compare the views of the people that you first interviewed about homelessness, the views you found in the newspapers, and your observations and discussions at the homeless shelter.

Option: essay

Write an essay (around four to five pages, typed) in which you discuss popular conceptions about homelessness with the realities of homelessness that you observed.

Option: bibliography

Use your library's indexes to construct a bibliography of ten to fifteen articles from social science journals or social science books that discuss the extent of homelessness in the United States today and the reasons for it. Type your bibliography in proper bibliographic style.

Option: research paper
Write a paper (around seven pages, typed) in which you discuss the nature of homelessness today, the reasons for it as offered by social scientists, and a comparison of social science explanations for homelessness and popular views about homelessness. Use at least five of the articles and/or books from your bibliography (above). Be sure to provide proper documentation throughout your paper and include a reference page.

NOTES:

CHAPTER 11

PREGNANCY: EXPERIENCES AND CHOICES

CHAPTER OUTLINE

Stages of Pregnancy
- First Trimester
- Second Trimester
- Third Trimester

Childbirth
- Coached Childbirth
- Childbirth Preparation
- Promoting Bonding
- Home Birth

The Postpartum Period
- Causes of Postpartum Depression
- Sexuality
- Breast-Feeding

Overview of Teen Pregnancy
- Who is at Risk?
- Long-Term Consequences

Explaining Racial and Ethnic Differences
- African-American Teen Pregnancy
- Mexican-American Teen Pregnancy
- Economic Issues

Involuntary Infertility

Adoption
- Unrelated Adoptions
- Interracial Adoption
- Foster-Adopt Program
- Foreign Adoptions

Voluntary Childlessness

Substance Abuse and Pregnancy

- Child Protective Services
- Inadequate Treatment Facilities
- Drug Abuse and Fetal AIDS Exposure

Abortion

- Early Abortions
- Late Abortions
- Safety
- Emotional Reactions
- Access to Abortion is Diminishing

CHAPTER LEARNING OBJECTIVES

After studying this chapter, you should be able to:

- identify and discuss the stages of pregnancy;
- discuss childbirth preparation and the advantages and disadvantages of different settings for childbirth;
- discuss the symptoms and causes of postpartum depression;
- discuss the advantages and concerns associated with breast-feeding;
- discuss the risk factors associated with teen pregnancy and the long-term consequences of teen pregnancy;
- identify and discuss factors that account for racial and ethnic differences in teenage pregnancy rates;
- discuss the impact of involuntary infertility on young married couples;
- identify and discuss five different types of adoption;
- identify and discuss the stages that a couple typically goes through when they drift into voluntary childlessness;

• discuss the biological and sociological problems related to substance abuse and pregnancy;

• discuss the extent to which abortions in the United States take place, who is most likely to have them, and when in the pregnancy they are most likely to occur;

• identify and discuss various methods of abortion, when during the pregnancy they are most likely to be used, and the relative safety or danger of each;

• discuss the political and legal realities of abortion.

KEY POINTS FOR REVIEW

• The duration of pregnancy is typically divided into three trimesters, each of which presents physiological changes, attitude changes, and different levels of comfort and discomfort. During the first trimester, physiological changes include tender breasts, the need to urinate frequently and "morning sickness" (nausea and vomiting). The couple typically experiences ambivalence about their future roles as parents. Sexual activity tends to decrease.

• In the second trimester morning sickness tends to disappear and the woman experiences a greater sense of well-being. Questions about their future roles as husband and wife and the woman's career emerge. While women often are concerned about their sexual attractiveness during this stage, vasocongestion in the pelvic area may contribute to enhanced arousal for them. Additionally, the couple does not have to worry about contraception, which also may lead to increased sexual activity. Often, couples experiment with new sexual positions and variations in their sexual practices during this stage.

• In the third trimester the woman typically experiences an increase in physical discomforts. The husband and wife experience anxiety about the delivery, the health of the infant, and the prospects of having in-laws and other relatives interfere. These anxieties often lead to a decrease in sexual activity during this stage.

• Having a partner or childbirth coach has important emotional benefits for the mother and newborn infant. A greater level of bonding between mother and child and father and child tends to occur where mothers had a partner present during delivery. Additionally, fathers who are present at the birth of their children tend to be more involved in child care after the delivery.

• The Lamaze method of childbirth is based on Fernand Lamaze's view that psychological preparation for childbirth could reduce the need for pain-killing drugs. Through Lamaze training, pregnant women are taught relaxation exercises aimed at keeping their muscles limp while the uterus is tense with contractions, thus reducing the amount of pain. This is done primarily through the use of breathing exercises.

• During the postpartum period—the period following childbirth—new mothers often experience postpartum depression. The causes of postpartum depression are a combination of physiological, psychological, and social factors. Because many women have an episiotomy—an incision under the vagina which helps the woman give birth easier—it is often recommended that the couple abstain from sexual intercourse for a period until it heals.

• There has been a revival of interest in breast-feeding in recent years because of the benefits it provides to the infant.

• About one million teenagers become pregnant each year. Approximately two-thirds of these are to unmarried mothers. The teenagers who are most at risk for bearing a child out of wedlock are those in low-income families who grow up in single-parent homes, live in the inner cities, have friends who are sexually active, and perform poorly in school.

• A longitudinal study of 300 teenage mothers in Baltimore found that the majority of them finished high school, left welfare, and found a regular job. However, they were worse off economically than their peers from similar backgrounds who avoided teen pregnancy. Additionally, high rates of school failure, delinquency, and teen pregnancy were found among the teenage children of these women.

• The percent of non-marital teen births is much higher among African Americans than among either whites or other racial groups because of reasons related to social class, racial discrimination, and cultural factors. African Americans are over-represented among the poor. The results of a shortage of employed African American men that can support a family are that African-American women have limited marriage prospects and have an increased likelihood of forming families through non-marital childbearing. Discrimination against African Americans—and the discouragement about the future—often leads female African-American adolescents to make less of an effort to avoid pregnancy. The lower class cultural ecology in which many African Americans live—including the school environment and sexual attitudes—raises the probability that teens will become pregnant.

• African Americans have less puritanical attitudes toward sex, are more open and accepting of sexuality, and have fewer problems both before and after marriage than whites. African American teens tend to begin sexual intercourse earlier than other groups and are therefore at greater risk of early parenthood.

• Mexican-American teenagers are less likely than non-Hispanic whites to have sexual intercourse. However, when Mexican-American teens are sexually active, they are less likely than non-Hispanic whites to use contraception and more likely to become pregnant. Hispanics are less likely than whites and African Americans to have an abortion.

• Involuntary infertility places great stress on young married couples who desire children. They may experience a decrease in the frequency of intercourse and sexual satisfaction, a loss of self-confidence, and feelings of sadness, depression, anger confusion, desperation, and embarrassment. This is often accompanied by "boundary confusion"—not knowing where the boundaries of the family lie.

• American couples adopt slightly over 100,000 American born children each year and an additional 9,000 children who were born outside of the United States. In half of all domestic adoptions, the adoptive parents are relatives of the child. The other half of domestic adoptions are unrelated adoptions. Most adoption occurs through public and private agencies. Some couples reduce their waiting time by seeking independent adoptions through lawyers or doctors. There is an increasing number of interracial and foreign adoptions. Recently, foster-adopt programs that place children with special needs in adoptive homes have become popular.

• There are four stages that a couple typically goes through when they drift into voluntary childlessness: agreeing to postpone childbearing for a specific amount of time, postponing childbearing to an indefinite time, considering the possibility of never having children, and reaching a conclusion that they definitely will not have children.

• Heavy exposure to alcohol and exposure to illicit drugs can result in serious physical problems and learning disabilities for the child. Some have argued for greater child protective services that would provide hospitals with the power to retain drug-exposed babies, deny incapable drug-addicted parents to have custody of their children, and liberalize adoption procedures to enable children with drug abusing parents to be placed with adoptive parents. Others argue that placing African-American children of drug-abusing parents in homes of white foster parents, which is often the case, is destructive to the African-American family and often causes drug-addicted mothers to avoid social services.

• There are not enough facilities for the treatment of drug abuse, which places babies of drug-addicted parents at further risk of child abuse. Since most drug-abusing females are sexually active, they run a higher risk of acquiring and exposing the fetus to AIDS.

• There are around 1.6 million abortions performed in the United States each year. The median age for women who obtain an abortion is twenty-three. African-American women are two and one-half times more likely than white women to have an abortion. Most abortions take place during the first trimester of pregnancy with a procedure known as suction curretage. Very few abortions are performed during the second trimester. At that point, either saline induction or dilation and evacuation are typically used. Complications rarely occur with abortions that are performed during the first trimester of pregnancy. For women who freely choose a legal abortion, serious negative emotional consequences are rare. Negative reactions are more likely among women who are very young, deeply religious, have experienced a recent breakup with a boyfriend, or who have been coerced into having an abortion.

• Even though abortion is legal for most people, access to abortion is diminishing. This is largely due to the desire on the part of hospitals and doctors to avoid the harassment of right-to-life groups. Abortion laws are regularly challenged and the laws regarding abortion are facing increasing scrutiny as the tensions between pro-choice and right-to-life groups escalate.

NOTES:

KEY TERMS

The following key terms are found in your textbook on the page number indicated in parentheses. In the space provided, write a brief definition of the key term. Then provide an example of the term, such as a culture in which the practice takes place, or people that you might know whose behavior illustrates the term. You could include issues that you might have read about in the news or in a book, or anything else that will illustrate the term and help you remember it. Include any comments from your class discussions or textbook that might help you remember and understand these key terms.

trimester (p. 291)

____

____

____

ambivalence (p. 291)

____

____

____

madonna complex (p. 292)

____

____

____

coached childbirth (p. 294)

____

____

childbirth preparation (p. 296)

home birth (p. 297)

postpartum period (p. 297)

postpartum depression (p. 297)

opportunity costs (p. 301)

social networks (p. 301)

cultural ecology (p. 305)

longitudinal study (p. 302)

racially isolated classroom (p. 305)

three-tier adoption policy (p. 308)

children with special needs (p. 308)

foster-adopt program (p. 308)

fetal alcohol syndrome (p. 311)

criminalization of illegal drug use during pregnancy (p. 312)

suction curettage (p. 313)

saline induction (p. 314)

dilation and evacuation (p. 314)

Roe vs. Wade decision (p. 315)

undue burden test (p. 316)

Webster decision (p. 316)

pro-life (p. 316)

pro-choice (p. 316)

NOTES:

PRACTICE TEST

Multiple Choice

1. During the first trimester of pregnancy, the couple typically:
   a) faces no fears at the prospect of being new parents
   b) expresses regret about the decision to have a baby
   c) experiences mixed and conflicting feelings about parenthood
   d) represses the fact that the wife is pregnant

2. During the first trimester of pregnancy, sexual activity tends to:
   a) decrease
   b) increase
   c) remain the same as before
   d) be much more creative

3. The madonna complex:
   a) makes it difficult for some partners of pregnant women to become sexually aroused
   b) leads to greater sexual arousal for husbands of pregnant women
   c) is when women feel an awakened and more uninhibited sexuality because of the constant attention they receive
   d) occurs when men feel jealous of the attention that the fetus is receiving

4. Pregnancy is often a time of elevated sexual pleasure during the second trimester because of all of the following except:
   a) the woman experiences vasocongestion in the pelvic area
   b) the couple does not have to worry about contraception
   c) the couple experiments with different sexual positions and techniques due to the inconvenience of using traditional positions
   d) a greater amount of testosterone is produced in males

5. For the expecting couple, the third trimester tends:
   a) to be a period of calm anticipation and joy at the prospects of being new parents
   b) to be a period of anxiety over the prospects of parenthood and the birth experience
   c) to be a period in which the couple has fully come to grips with their new roles
   d) to be a period in which the couple goes through a stage of denial

6. The Lamaze method of childbirth is based on French obstetrician Fernand Lamaze's reasoning that:
   a) being tense and frightened can cause greater pain to the woman during childbirth
   b) strengthening a woman's pelvic muscles can help her to give birth quicker
   c) giving a woman drugs during childbirth is actually the best way to keep her calm
   d) the presence of the husband tends to increase the wife's level of anxiety

7. The basic techniques taught during Lamaze preparation for childbirth are:
   a) how to use breathing techniques to relax
   b) how to use drugs effectively and safely in order to relax
   c) how to identify which areas of the body are in pain so that the woman can request specific forms of anesthesia
   d) how to make certain muscles tense in order to distract from the pain of childbirth

8. During the postpartum period:
   a) the mother often goes through a period of depression for a few days or weeks
   b) the mother usually experiences a natural high and an elevated mood for a few days or weeks
   c) the level of communication between the couple generally decreases
   d) the father usually develops phantom symptoms associated with childbirth

9. Sexual activity between the couple during the immediate postpartum period:
   a) usually increases because of the stronger bond created between the partners
   b) usually decreases because of physical discomfort that the mother experiences
   c) usually increases because of the tension associated with childbirth
   d) usually decreases because of the natural production of a male hormone designed to protect the woman and insure more attention to the newborn child

10. In many cultures, during the woman's pregnancy the father goes through the "couvade" in which he:
    a) experiences some of the physical, psychological, and emotional symptoms that mother's typically experience
    b) cuts himself off from his friends and family for a period of time in order to prepare the home for the new child
    c) goes through a period of daily prayer and other religious rituals
    d) develop breasts

11. Approximately how many teenagers become pregnant each year in the United States?
    a) 50,000
    b) 500,000
    c) 1 million
    d) 5 million

12. Of live births to teenagers in the United States each year, approximately how many are to unmarried mothers?
   a) 15 percent
   b) 33 percent
   c) 66 percent
   d) 80 percent

13. Of the following, who is at the most risk for bearing a child out of wedlock?
   a) middle class teenagers who live in the suburbs
   b) teenagers who are active in extracurricular school activities
   c) teenagers who have friends that are not very sexually active
   d) teenagers from low-income families who grow up in single-parent homes

14. To say that the opportunity costs of teen pregnancy are low for some teenagers means:
   a) that it is easy for some teenagers to find someone with whom they can be sexually active
   b) some teenagers feel that they are giving up very little by becoming pregnant
   c) medical care is less expensive for teenagers giving birth than for adults
   d) it is easy for unmarried teenagers to get welfare

15. Which of the following groups of teenagers are most likely to become pregnant?
   a) teenagers who see prospects of a good job and a bright economic future
   b) teenagers who have low educational and occupational aspirations
   c) teenagers who have friends who are sexually inexperienced
   d) teenagers who are emotionally stable and have a sense of independence

16. Teen pregnancy occurs most often among:
   a) whites
   b) Mexican Americans
   c) Japanese Americans
   d) African Americans

17. Because African Americans have less puritanical attitudes toward sex than whites, they tend to:
   a) have more problems with sex than whites both before and after marriage
   b) have fewer problems with sex than whites both before and after marriage
   c) be more likely than whites to use contraceptives
   d) be more likely than whites to undergo voluntary sterilization

18. In a study of 207 low-income African American youth in mother-headed families cited in your textbook, the majority reported that:
   a) they were abandoned by their fathers

b) they had poor relationships with their fathers
c) they had positive relationships with their fathers
d) their mother and father had a poor relationship with each other

19. "Boundary confusion" is most likely to occur among:
    a) couples that are involuntarily infertile
    b) families where there is an adopted child
    c) teenage parents
    d) all unmarried parents

20. Approximately how many American born children are adopted in the United States each year?
    a) 10,000
    b) 50,000
    c) 100,000
    d) 500,000

21. Most adoptions in the United States:
    a) take place through public and private agencies
    b) are independent adoptions which are made through lawyers and doctors
    c) are interracial and foreign adoptions
    d) are through foster-adopt programs

22. One reason that interracial adoptions are increasing is because:
    a) it has become increasingly politically correct to adopt a children outside of one's race
    b) it is less expensive to adopt African-American children
    c) low income African American and Native American mothers feel that their children would have better life chances in middle class white families
    d) the number of couples seeking to adopt an infant is far greater than the number of babies available for adoption

23. The typical stages that couples who drift into voluntary childlessness include all of the following except:
    a) agreeing to postpone childbearing for a definite period of time
    b) agreeing to postpone childbearing for an indefinite period of time
    c) considering the possibility of never having children
    d) becoming permanently ambivalent about the possibility of having children

24. Which of the following drugs is not detrimental to the fetus?
   a) alcohol
   b) marijuana
   c) cocaine
   d) all drugs pose risks for the fetus

25. Approximately how many abortions occur in the United States each year?
   a) 50,000
   b) 500,000
   c) 1.5 million
   d) 5 million

26. The United States abortion rate is:
   a) the lowest of all industrialized nations in the world
   b) much higher than that in other developed countries
   c) about the same as in other developed countries
   d) decreasing much more rapidly than in other developed countries

27. Which of the following is (are) true about people's attitudes toward abortion:
   a) African-American women disapprove of abortion more than white women
   b) African-American men disapprove of abortion more than white men
   c) African-American women disapprove of abortion more than African-American men
   d) a and c

28. The most common method of abortion performed in the United States is:
   a) suction curettage
   b) saline induction
   c) dilation and evacuation
   d) diffusion

29. The safest abortion procedure is:
   a) suction curettage
   b) saline induction
   c) dilation and evacuation
   d) currently no abortion procedure is without significant physical and emotional risk to the mother

30. The "undue burden" test established by the U.S. Supreme Court states that:
   a) an undue burden should not be placed on the potential health of the unborn fetus
   b) an undue burden should not be imposed on a woman's abortion decision
   c) an undue burden is sufficient reason for a woman to have an abortion
   d) an undue burden is insufficient reason for a woman to have an abortion

PROJECTS

PROJECT 11. 1 Examining Attitudes Toward Abortion

Even though the United States has the highest rate of abortions performed than any other developed country, abortion continues to grow as a controversial issue. The confrontations between pro-life and pro-choice groups seem to be increasing. Often, people's views about controversial issues such as abortion can be guided more by emotions than by reason. The objective of this activity is to have you examine both sides of the abortion debate from a rational, rather than an emotional, point of view.

Journal instructions:

1. Interview three people on your campus or in your community that are firm "pro-life" advocates and three people who are firm "pro-choice" advocates. For each, record in your journal their gender, race, highest level of education, religion, occupation, marital status, age, and income level (if possible). Ask them the following questions and record their answers in your journal:
   a) Why do you feel abortion should be illegal or legal?
   b) What do you feel are the major considerations in the debate over legalized abortion?
   c) Why do you think the debate is so controversial and why does it persist?
   d) What are your views about pre-marital sex?
   e) Personally, considering your own circumstances, do you feel that sex is primarily for procreation or for pleasure, or both?
   f) Do you feel that women should be equal to men in rights and responsibilities in the family?
   g) Do you feel that women should have the same employment opportunities as men?
   h) Who do you think primarily should be responsible for taking care of the children in the family: father, mother, both?

2. In your journal, summarize and analyze the responses to the interviews you conducted.

3. In newspapers or news magazines, locate five letters-to-the-editor, editorials, essays, or opinion articles that advocate pro-choice and five that advocate pro-life. For each, summarize the source of the argument being made. Is it based on facts, evidence, emotion, personal experience, or anything else. Record these and the periodical information in your journal.

4. Based upon your interviews and the opinions you found in the newspapers or magazines, what types of arguments are generally made from the pro-choice and the pro-life positions? Are there any common characteristics of people who take each position? If so, what are they? Do the positions tend to be based upon facts or upon emotions? Discuss these questions in your journal.

Option: essay

1. Re-read the section in Chapter 2 of Robin Wolf's *Marriage and Family* that discusses theories of the family. Additionally, read the section about major theoretical perspectives in sociology from any introduction to sociology textbook.

2. Write an essay (around five pages, typed) in which you discuss the abortion controversy from the point of view of the sociological theories found in Wolf and in the introductory text. In other words, how would each of the theories explain the abortion controversy? Use material from your journal exercise, above, to illustrate the theories.

Option: bibliography

Develop a bibliography of ten articles from the *Reader's Guide to Periodical Literature* and ten articles from the *Social Science Index* within the past few years that contain debates or discussions about the abortion controversy. Type your bibliography using the format found in your textbook or in one of the social science journal articles.

Option: research paper

1. From your bibliography (above), select four articles from popular magazines and four articles from social science journals that contain discussions about the abortion controversy. Be sure to select articles that provide you with arguments for and against legalized abortion. Read the articles you select and outline the reasons they provide for and/or against keeping abortion legal.

2. Using the information from your journal activity (previous page) and library research, write a paper (around seven pages, typed) in which you present well-organized arguments for keeping abortion legal and for making abortion illegal. Use the theoretical perspectives you examined in the essay activity (above) as a framework to organize the data that you have collected and to develop your positions for and against legalized abortion. **Be sure to leave your personal feelings and emotions out of the positions for and against legalized abortion, and provide a balanced debate.** After you provide a balanced discussion of the reasons for and against legalized abortion, take a position **using information you obtained while doing this project**. Be sure to support your position with facts, not emotions. Provide proper documentation of your references throughout your paper and include a reference page.

NOTES:

PROJECT 11. 2 Exploring Methods of Childbirth

As Wolf mentions in Chapter 11, there are a variety of ways and settings in which people choose to give birth. Sometimes, reading about an experience cannot fully convey what it is like. The objective of this activity is to have you gain a solid sense of what the different methods and settings of childbirth offer for the parents before, during, and after the birth of the child, and for the child when it is born.

Journal instructions:

1. Interview a counselor from a family planning center, an obstetrician, a nurse, and, if possible, a midwife. Ask them to identify, explain, and discuss the advantages and disadvantages of the different types of care providers, childbirth settings, childbirth methods, participation of relatives or significant others, and postpartum activities. Record these interviews in your journal.

2. Interview three couples who are in the stages of childbirth preparation. If you cannot interview the couples, interview at least the mother-to-be. Ask them which methods and settings of childbirth that they selected and why. Record these interviews in your journal.

3. Attend and observe two childbirth classes. You can find out where these are being held from a local hospital or family planning center. In your journal, record as much as you can about the classes. Include descriptions of things such as the types of people that attend, the way that the rooms are set up, the subject-matter of the classes, the questions that people ask, the activities that occur as part of the class, and so on. Take rich, detailed notes about as much as you can during your observations.

4. Interview three couples (or mothers) who have given childbirth in different settings or using different methods (using natural childbirth methods, traditional methods, midwife, and so on). Ask them about the advantages and disadvantages about the method, setting, care-provider, and post-partum activities they experienced, and whether or not they would do it the same way if the were to have another child. Record these interviews in your journal.

Option: essay

Write an essay (around three to five pages, typed) in which you discuss and evaluate the types of childbirth settings, methods, care-providers, and postpartum activities that you learned about from your observations and interviews. As part of your essay, discuss the ways you (or you and your spouse) would (or will) chose to give birth.

Option: bibliography
Use the library's indexes (*Social Science Index, Reader's Guide to Periodical Literature,* or others) to develop a bibliography of fifteen to twenty articles from social science journals and popular periodicals about childbirth methods, settings, care-providers,and postpartum activities. Obtain a good balance of articles from social science journals and popular periodicals. Type your bibliography following the format in the social science journals or in your textbook.

Option: research paper
Write a paper (around seven to nine pages, typed) in which you compare the different methods, settings, care-providers, and postpartum experiences that are available for childbirth. Present a balanced view of each approach, discussing the advantages and disadvantages of each, based upon your library research and illustrated with information (observations and interviews) you collected in your journal activity (above). Use at least five sources from your bibliography, at least three of which must be from social science journals. Be sure to provide proper documentation of your sources throughout your paper and include a works cited page.

CHAPTER 12

PARENTS AND CHILDREN

CHAPTER OUTLINE

Socialization and Parenting Styles
- Parenting Styles
- Consistency
- Problems with Authoritarian Parenting

Positive Parenting
- Time-Out
- Natural Consequences
- Logical Consequences
- Creating a Consensual Environment

Relationships with Peers

The Growing Role of Fathers
- Father-Child Involvement
- Marital Satisfaction and Fathering

Balancing Parenting and Employment

One-Parent Families
- Single Parents and the Perceptions of Control
- Transition from a Two-Parent to a One-Parent Family
- Parenting Problems
- Benefits of Growing up in a One-Parent Family
- The Importance of the Non-custodial Father

Adoption
- Closed Adoption
- Open Adoption
- Searching for Birth Parents

Teenagers as Parents
- Stress in Teen Parenting
- Teenage Parents and Their Mothers

Immigrant Parents
Vietnamese-American Parents
Hispanic-American Parents

Adult Children as Caregivers
Sandwiched Generation
Stages of Caregiving
Continuity in the Caregiving Role
Strain in Caregiving
Racial Differences in Caregiving

CHAPTER LEARNING OBJECTIVES

After studying this chapter, you should be able to:

- identify and discuss three basic parenting styles;
- evaluate three basic parenting styles and discuss which are likely to be the most effective;
- identify and discuss positive parenting alternatives to spanking;
- discuss how parenting style influences the behavior of children in their relationship with their peers;
- identify and discuss three fathering styles and factors associated with the quantity and quality of a father's involvement with his children;
- discuss some ways in which parents balance child-rearing and employment in the United States;
- identify and discuss some discipline-related issues in divorced, one parent families;
- discuss the benefits of growing up in a one-parent family;
- discuss the differences between closed and open adoption;
- discuss the development of children born to teenage parents;
- identify and discuss four models of mother-grandmother relationships in the families of unwed teens;
- discuss the special problems that immigrant parents face as they attempt to raise children in the United States;
- discuss the ways in which children act as caregivers to their parents in the United States;
- discuss the strains that exist for women who act as caregivers to their parents and to their ill husbands;
- discuss racial differences in caregiving.

KEY POINTS FOR REVIEW

• Socialization is the process by which a society passes on its behavior patterns, attitudes, values, and knowledge to the next generation. The socialization process is affected largely by the type of parenting style enacted within the family. The different parenting styles reflect the different ways parents exercise punishment and discipline. Punishment is a reaction to the child's behavior which results in deprivation or pain. Discipline encompasses the various ways parents guide the behavior and attitudes of children. Three parenting styles are permissive, authoritarian, and authoritative.

• Permissive parents set few rules and make very few demands on children. The focus is on being responsive to the needs and wishes of the children. Children are expected to regulate their own behavior and the children are seen as having equal, or nearly equal, rights to those of adults. This approach involves very little punishment and discipline.

• Authoritarian parents set rigid rules for children and demand compliance. The emphasis is on obedience enforced through punishment. Children are seen as having very few rights as compared to adults. Authoritarian parenting often creates power struggles between parents and children and tends to inhibit the development of the child's conscience.

• Authoritative parents attempt to balance their demands and responses to the needs of the child. They set firm rules for behavior and enforce those rules, yet encourage children to make some decisions on their own. Punishment is not emphasized, but will occur if the child does not comply. The emphasis instead is on discussing behavior with the child. Both parents and children are seen as having rights that need to be respected. Authoritative parenting tends to enable parents to provide more consistent style of discipline than permissive or authoritarian parenting.

• Positive child guidance uses alternatives to spanking which include time-out, natural consequences, logical consequences, and creating a consensual environment. In "time-out" the disruptive child is removed from the situation for enough time to allow the child to calm down. "Natural consequences," which works best if the child is not disruptive, refers to allowing children to make their own choices and suffer the consequences of those choices. "Logical consequences" are consequences that the parent creates that grow logically out of the child's misdeed. In creating a "consensual environment" the emphasis is on cooperation rather than on a power struggle between parents and children.

• Parenting style affects the behavior of children. Parents who express warmth and are emotionally available to their children tend to have children with fewer behavioral problems than parents who are cold and rejecting. Parents who use coercive discipline tend to have children who are less preferred by their peers as playmates. Parents who use inductive reasoning to discipline their children tend to have children who get along well with their playmates. In addition, discipline styles affect the development of a child's problem-solving skills. In general, children of parents who used inductive reasoning in discipline preferred "friendly assertive" problem-solving strategies with their peers.

• The role of fathers in child-rearing is increasing in both single-headed families and in two-parent families. The father-headed one-parent families is the fastest growing family form. One account of fathering distinguishes between three types of fathering based upon levels of involvement between fathers and children. "Accessible fathers" spend time doing chores near their children but do not often engage in one-to-one interaction. "Engaged fathers" spend time talking and playing with their children. "Responsible fathers" go beyond interacting with their children and take responsibility for essential activities such as making doctor's appointments and arranging for baby-sitters.

• Factors associated with father-child involvement generally include the father's gender role orientation and marital satisfaction. Androgynous fathers take a larger role in parenting than fathers with traditional sex role characteristics. Fathers who experience higher marital satisfaction are more involved with their children than fathers who are not as satisfied in their marriage.

• A major concern for parents who are employed outside the home is finding quality child care for their children. Most preschool children of employed parents are cared for in their own family home or in someone else's. The second most used method of child care is a day care center. The majority of grade school and junior high school children of employed parents are latchkey children.

• An important source of stress for single parents is the necessity of guiding or disciplining children. Single mothers who perceive themselves as being in control of their families tend to be successful parents. Single parents tend to have more discipline problems with boys than with girls. This is especially true of divorced mothers.

• After divorce the parenting style of the custodial parent affects the ease with which children make the transition from a two-parent to a one-parent family. Divorced parents who use an authoritative parenting style based on warmth and firmness tend to have children who exhibit social competence with low levels of peer conflict.

• Children in one-parent families tend to be more androgynous than children in two-parent families. Children of single parents also exhibit greater maturity and a stronger sense of self efficacy.

• After a divorce, the relationship children have with their non-custodial parent has an important effect on their sense of well-being. Regular visits with the non-custodial parent as well as with extended kin on both sides of the family is associated with optimism, better self-concepts, and higher levels of aspiration and achievement in school. However, the critical relationship for the child's post-divorce emotional adjustment is with the custodial parent.

• In a closed adoption, the birth mother does not meet the adoptive parents or have any identifying information about them. In an open adoption, the birth mother typically meets the adoptive parents and approves of them before relinquishing her child for adoption.

• Children born to teenage mothers are at higher risk for developmental delays than children born to older parents. Extended kin networks often provide emotional and instrumental support to teen parents. There are a number of models of mother-grandmother relationships in the families of unwed teens. In the "parent replacement model" the grandmother assumes responsibility for child-rearing while her daughter plays a minimal role. In the "supplement model" the young mother and her mother share child care. In the "supported parent model" the young mother takes full responsibility for child care and receives help from her mother only when necessary. In the "apprentice model" the young mother takes full responsibility for child care under the close supervision of her mother.

• Immigrant parents face unique problems as they struggle to raise their children in the United States. Immigrant Vietnamese-American families fear that the encroachment of American culture into their family life may erode parental authority and the value of familism. Immigrant Hispanic-American children have been taught values, such as cooperation rather than competition, which often impede their chances for success in American schools.

• Medical technology has extended life expectancy. Thus, the number of elderly persons that have to be cared for by their adult children is growing. Many modern mid-life couples are part of the "sandwiched generation" because they are raising children at the same time they are caring for disabled and aging parents. Adult daughters tend to ease into a caregiving role with their parents, providing care before the parent becomes dependent. Some elderly mothers are self-sufficient, depending on their children primarily for transportation. Others are dependent and need help with many areas of their personal lives.

• The caregiving role tends to put a strain on a marriage. Adult daughters who provide care for an elderly parent are likely to have more marital difficulties, more disagreements with their spouses, and higher levels of depression than non-caregivers. Adult women who care for their parents have a higher sense of well-being than adult women who care for their ill-husbands.

• African-American families are less likely than white families to involve the elderly relative in decisions about that relative's care.

KEY TERMS

The following key terms are found in your textbook on the page number indicated in parentheses. In the space provided, write a brief definition of the key term. Then provide an example of the term, such as a culture in which the practice takes place, or people that you might know whose behavior illustrates the term. You could include issues that you might have read about in the news or in a book, or anything else that will illustrate the term and help you remember it. Include any comments from your class discussions or textbook that might help you remember and understand these key terms.

socialization (p. 322)

____

____

____

discipline (p. 322)

____

____

____

permissive parenting (p. 323)

____

____

____

authoritarian parenting (p. 323)

____

____

consistency (p. 324)

power struggles (p. 324)

functionally superfluous control (p. 326)

time-out (p. 326)

natural consequences (p. 326)

logical consequences (p. 327)

consensual environment (p. 327)

coercive discipline (p. 328)

inductive reasoning (p. 328)

instrumental support (p. 339)

"off-time"parenting (p. 339)

parent replacement model (p. 340)

supplement model (p. 340)

supported parent model (p. 340)

apprentice model (p. 341)

familism (p. 341)

compadres (p. 343)

role reversal (p. 345)

sandwiched generation (p. 345)

NOTES:

PRACTICE TEST

Multiple Choice

1. The term that social scientists use for the process by which a society passes on its behavior patterns, attitudes, values, and knowledge to the next generation is:
   a) parenting
   b) socialization
   c) transmission
   d) learning

2. A person's overall approach to parenting usually revolves around a parent's use of:
   a) punishment
   b) discipline
   c) rewards
   d) socialization

3. Which of the following statements about punishment and discipline is true?
   a) punishment is a broad concept that encompasses the various ways parents guide children
   b) discipline is a broad concept that encompasses the various ways parents guide children
   c) discipline is a reaction to the child's behavior which results in deprivation or pain
   d) punishment is more effective than discipline

4. Which parenting style emphasizes discussing behavior with the child, de-emphasizes punishment, yet includes punishment of children when necessary?
   a) permissive
   b) authoritarian
   c) authoritative
   d) dogmatic

5. In authoritarian child-rearing, parents:
   a) attempt to balance demands and parental responsiveness to the needs of the child
   b) set firm rules for appropriate behavior, but foster individuality by encouraging children to make some decisions on their own
   c) set rigid rules for children and make strong demands for their compliance with these rules
   d) set few rules and make very few demands on children

6. Which parenting style is most likely to produce parental consistency with regard to discipline?
   a) permissive
   b) authoritarian
   c) authoritative
   d) dogmatic

7. The use of inconsistent discipline by parents is associated with:
   a) problems in the relationship between children and their peers
   b) higher self-esteem among children
   c) greater sense of individuality among children
   d) stronger conscience among children

8. Which parenting style is most likely to result in power struggles between parents and children?
   a) permissive
   b) authoritarian
   c) authoritative
   d) dogmatic

9. The "logical consequences" approach to parenting involves:
   a) presenting the child with a choice of engaging in acceptable behavior or having limits placed on the unacceptable behavior
   b) allowing children to make their own choices and suffer the consequences of those choices
   c) creating an environment of cooperation between parents and child
   d) removing the disruptive child from the situation to allow the child time to calm down

10. In parent-child relationships that emphasize punishment, children tend:
    a) to develop a self-centered view of the world
    b) to become overly concerned with the needs of others
    c) to become more cooperative
    d) to value independence and intellectual activity

11. Children raised in a consensual environment are more likely to:
    a) become egocentric
    b) have difficulty learning to make decisions on their own
    c) have difficulty with peer relationships
    d) be more cooperative and comply with parents

12. Which statement by a parent is most characteristic of inductive reasoning as a means of discipline?
    a) "Don't call Bobby names unless you want a spanking."
    b) "If you continue to call Bobby names you will be put in time-out."
    c) "When you call Bobby names, it hurts his feelings."
    d) "You can call Bobby names if you want, but if you do you will be punished."

13. Which type of discipline style tends to increase the likelihood children using "friendly-assertive" problem-solving strategies with their peers?
a) coercive discipline
b) inductive reasoning
c) authoritarian parenting
d) there is no relationship between discipline style and children's problem-solving strategies

14. The fastest growing family form is:
a) the mother-headed one-parent family
b) the father-headed one-parent family
c) two-parent families with fathers who take primary responsibility for children
d) the traditional two-parent family where the mother takes primary responsibility for children

15. The father doing chores near the child but not often engaging in one-to-one interaction with the child most nearly describes which fathering style identified by social scientists?
a) accessible fathers
b) engaged fathers
c) disengaged fathers
d) responsible fathers

16. Which factor is most directly associated with a father's willingness to spend time with his children?
a) his income
b) his occupation
c) his gender role orientation
d) his level of education

17. Studies show that a spouse's level of marital satisfaction influences parenting behavior in which of the following ways?
a) fathers who were experiencing marital difficulties spent less time with their children than fathers who were satisfied with their marriage
b) fathers who were satisfied with their marriage spent less time with their children than fathers who were having marital difficulties
c) fathers whose love for their mates had declined behaved more positively toward their children than fathers who experienced marital satisfaction
d) mothers who experienced marital difficulties spent less time with their children than mothers who are satisfied with their marriage

18. Studies show that single mothers who perceived themselves as being in control of the parent-child relationship tended to:
a) have more rebellious children
b) have children who try to exercise more control over their peers
c) had less success in parenting than mothers who viewed the child as having significant control in the relationship
d) had greater success in parenting than mothers who viewed the child as having significant control in the relationship

19. Children in single-parent families:
a) tend to be more androgynous than children in two-parent homes
b) tend to adhere to more traditional gender roles than children in two-parent homes
c) tend to mature at a slower rate than children in two-parent homes
d) tend to have a lower sense of self-efficacy than children in two-parent homes

20. With regard to personal development, teenage mothers tend:
a) to mature quicker emotionally than their peers that do not have children because of their increased responsibilities
b) to experience a postponement of their own development because of their increased responsibilities
c) spend more time than their peers without children planning for their future
d) to be no different emotionally, cognitively, or psychologically than their peers without children

21. Which model of mother-grandmother relationships that exists among unwed teen mothers is child care likely to have the least amount of intervention and support from the grandmother:
a) parent replacement model
b) supplement model
c) supported parent model
d) apprentice model

22. The most frequently used model of mother-grandmother relationships among unwed teen mothers is:
a) parent replacement model
b) supplement model
c) supported parent model
d) apprentice model

23. In which model of mother-grandmother relationships among unwed teen mothers are young mothers most likely to have the best chance to develop parenting skills:
a) parent replacement model
b) supplement model
c) supported parent model
d) apprentice model

24. Both Vietnamese and Hispanic immigrant parents are likely to feel that:
a) American children are socialized to be more selfish and competitive then they would like
b) American children are much more cooperative than they are used to
c) Americans have much greater familial support networks than their cultures
d) Americans are much more concerned for the collective good than in their cultures

25. With regard to adult caregiving for the elderly:
a) there are no significant differences between African-American and white families
b) white families are less likely than African-American families to involve the elderly relative in decisions about that relative's care
c) African-American families are less likely than white families to involve the elderly relative in decisions about that relative's care
d) more relatives tend to be involved in making decisions about the care of the elderly in African-American families than in white families

NOTES:

PROJECTS

PROJECT 12. 1 Observing Parenting Styles

In Chapter 12, Robin Wolf discusses a number of different socialization and parenting styles. These parenting styles are based mostly in the ways in which the parents use discipline. The style of parenting used by parents tends to have long term consequences for the ways in which children develop, perform in school, and relate to their peers. The objective of this activity is to help you recognize and become aware of the different styles of parenting and to give you practice in conducting field research.

Journal instructions:

1. Re-read the sections in Chapter 12 that discuss parenting styles and positive parenting. Note especially Table 12.1 and Box 12.1.

2. For one week, observe parenting styles in as many settings and during as many instances as possible: in your home, in the homes of friends and relatives, at a playground, in shopping malls and stores, at birthday parties, and so on. Keep detailed records of your observations in your journal. Use a separate page in your journal for each of your observations. On each observation note the following:
   a) the setting (in home, grocery store, playground, church, and so on)
   b) the nature of the interaction (parent is correcting a child for something, child is asking permission, child is misbehaving, and so on)
   c) descriptions of the type of discipline used (what the parents said or did)
   d) demands placed on the child (quantity and quality - see Table 12.1)
   e) degree to which the child's needs and wishes were responded to (see Table 12.1)
   f) extent to which child's and parent's respective rights are considered (see Table 12.1)
   g) level of coercion involved (see Table 12.1)
   h) amount of inductive reasoning (see Table 12.1)
   i) extent to which positive parenting methods were used (time-out, natural consequences, logical consequences, creating a consensual environment)

In addition, for each observation keep a record of the approximate ages of the children and parents, gender of the children and parents, race, and any other cues about the statuses of the people involved.

Hint: Before you begin your observations, create a sheet that includes a list of the above items to look for and space under each item so that you can write your observations. Make around twenty copies of these sheets and keep them available for you to use as needed during the week.

3. After each observation, write a brief analysis discussing the parenting style (permissive, authoritative, or authoritarian) that you feel was used and why you reached your conclusion.

Option: essay
Summarize the results of your field research (above) and write an essay (around three to five pages, typed) in which you discuss the parenting styles you observed. You can address such items as the effectiveness of the different parenting styles, whether or not parenting style depends upon the situation or the particular people involved, how your conclusions compare with those discussed by Robin Wolf, or any other item of interest of which you became aware during your observation research.

Option: bibliography
Develop a bibliography of ten articles from the *Reader's Guide to Periodical Literature* and ten articles from the *Social Science Index* within the past few years that contain debates or discussions about parenting styles. Type your bibliography using the format found in your textbook or in one of the social science journal articles.

Option: research paper
Use material from four or five articles from you bibliography (at least two should be from social science journals) and your observations (above) to write a paper (around five to seven pages, typed) in which you discuss the effectiveness and outcomes of different parenting styles. You can address such questions and issues as:

- Do different types of people use different parenting styles? If so, discuss.
- Does the setting make a difference in effectiveness of the parenting style?
- What are some examples of different parenting styles that you observed?
- Are your conclusions and observations supported by the articles you read? If so, how?
- Do your conclusions and observations support the conclusions made in the articles? If so, how?
- Do your conclusions and observations conflict with those in the articles? If so, how?
- Do you agree that there are only three parenting styles?
- Do people manifest only one parenting style or is it sometimes a combination of more than one?

You do not have to answer all of the above questions. Use them as suggestions for possible items to structure your paper around.

Provide proper documentation of your references throughout your paper and include a reference page.

NOTES:

CHAPTER 13

COMMUNICATION AND CONFLICT

CHAPTER OUTLINE

Communication
- Nonverbal Communication

Exchange Theory
- Empathy
- Appreciation

Conflict Theory
- Equal versus Traditional Partnerships

Symbolic Interaction Theory
- Communication and the Development of the Self

Communication Styles
- Non-assertion
- Aggressive Communication
- Assertion

Components of an Assertive Statement
- Bonding Statement
- "I" Statements
- The Conclusion to an Assertive Statement

Conflict and Family Roles
- Methods for Stopping Conflict
- Social Roles and Conflict

Communication Problems
- Invalidation
- Indirect Communication
- Manipulation
- Double Messages

CHAPTER LEARNING OBJECTIVES

After studying this chapter, you should be able to:

- discuss differences between communication, feedback, and non-verbal communication in a marriage;
- discuss the functions of conflict in a marriage;
- discuss how exchange theory explains the ways in which communication provides the glue that holds people together in family relationships;
- discuss how conflict theory explains communication as a source of power and how power influences communication patterns in a marriage;
- discuss how symbolic interaction theory explains the way that communication in the family affects people's perceptions of reality and the development of the self;
- identify, discuss, and distinguish between three major communication styles;
- identify and discuss three communication problems associated with non-assertive communication;
- identify and discuss four forms of aggressive communication;
- discuss the nature of assertive communication;
- identify and discuss the components of an assertive statement;
- discuss the part that family roles play in both conflict initiating and conflict management;
- identify and discuss four methods family members use to stop conflict;
- identify and discuss four types of communication problems.

KEY POINTS FOR REVIEW

• Communication style is an important predictor of marital success. Communication involves the sending and receiving of messages. One way to discern the impact of one's message on the other person is through feedback—a verbal or non-verbal response to a message. Non-verbal communication can act as a message within itself or it can frame a verbal statement. Non-verbal communication is often interpreted differently by two partners.

• Conflict refers to the exchange of opposing messages. The avoidance of conflict was recommended by marriage counselors fifty years ago. Social scientists today believe that conflicts, if expressed appropriately, has positive functions in a marriage, often leading to stronger feelings of love and intimacy.

• According to exchange theory, people remain in relationships when the benefits outweigh the costs. Many of the benefits and costs of a relationship are experienced through the process of communication. Spouses who rate their partners high on the expression of warmth tend to be satisfied with their marital relationships. The expression of empathy draws couple together and is associated with marital satisfaction. Likewise, children who express empathy toward their peers are sought out as friends more often than children who do not. The expression of appreciation tends to bond people together and provides rewards for the partner.

• Conflict theory holds that communication is often used to influence or dominate another person. To successfully influence the behavior of someone else is to exercise power. Those with greater resources have more power and can exert influence over their partners. Power is often displayed through aggressive communication that attempts to dominate and control the partner. Women in equal partnerships are more likely to use an assertive approach to communication with their husbands. Women in traditional partnerships, where the husband has more resources, tend to use indirect strategies in their communication.

• Symbolic interaction theory looks at the way communication uses words as symbols to label our experience and influence our perception of reality. Communication in families plays an important role in the development of a person's identity. Two important social theorists, Charles Horton Cooley and George Herbert Mead, have theorized how the self-concept—the image that we hold of ourselves—stems from the images that we think others have of us. The way people communicate with us, verbally and non-verbally, affects our self-concept.

• Three communication styles commonly used in conflict situations are non-assertion, aggression, and assertion. Non-assertion is a self-denying and passive form of communication. It is associated with three communication problems: gunnysacking—when the non-assertive communicator carries around grievances, allows them to build, and eventually explodes in irritation over a last-straw incident—the assumption of mind reading, and allowing the partner to define the situation as one in which the non-assertive partner is to blame.

• Aggressive communication involves expressing feelings, wants, ideas, and needs in a way that attempts to dominate, control, and even humiliate the partner. This typically takes the form of blaming, demeaning, making threats and giving orders, and coercive escalation—a series of attacks followed by counter-attacks.

• Assertion is the communication style most likely to successfully resolve a conflict. Partners who use assertive communication state feelings and wants directly, with honesty, and without depreciating other people.

• An empathetic assertive statement usually has three components: a bonding statement, "I"-statements, and a conclusion. A bonding statement shows a person values the relationship and wants it to continue. "I"-statements express a person's thoughts and feelings from a personal perspective and take ownership for their feelings. The conclusion to an assertive statement has three major uses: asking for what you want or need, saying "no" to a request, stating what you plan to do.

• Vuchinich identified four methods family members use to stop conflict: submission, compromise, withdrawal, and standoff. Vuchinich also found that there tends to be an overall egalitarian pattern of conflict initiation with all family members exhibiting conflict initiation rights. Mothers tend to play an important part in conflict management, followed by daughters.

• There are four types of communication problems. Invalidation involves convincing partners that their feelings are not valid and should not exist or be expressed, thus violating the other partner's right to be treated with respect. In indirect communication, speakers use hints and implied messages to state their thoughts. Manipulation involves indirect messages in a way that combines hints with an effort to control the partner's behavior. Double messages are two or more contradictory messages from a single person.

KEY TERMS

The following key terms are found in your textbook on the page number indicated in parentheses. In the space provided, write a brief definition of the key term. Then provide an example of the term, such as a culture in which the practice takes place, or people that you might know whose behavior illustrates the term. You could include issues that you might have read about in the news or in a book, or anything else that will illustrate the term and help you remember it. Include any comments from your class discussions or textbook that might help you remember and understand these key terms.

communication (p. 352)

____

____

____

feedback (p. 353)

____

____

____

conflict (p. 335)

____

____

____

exchange theory (p. 335)

____

____

empathy (p. 356)

conflict theory (p. 357)

symbolic interaction theory (p. 358)

non-assertion (p. 361)

gunnysacking (p. 361)

last-straw incident (p. 361)

assumption of mind-reading (p. 361)

definition of the situation (p. 361)

aggression (p. 362)

coercive escalation (p. 364)

assertion (p. 364)

"I"-statements (p. 365)

owning feelings (p. 368)

invalidation (p. 373)

indirect communication (p. 373)

manipulation (p. 374)

counter-manipulation (p. 374)

natural consequences (p. 375)

double messages (p. 375)

NOTES:

PRACTICE TEST

Multiple Choice

1. Which is the most important predictor of marital success?
   a) communication
   b) the amount of leisure time spent together
   c) family finances
   d) the sexual relationship

2. Generally speaking, the expression of conflict within a marriage:
   a) is usually destructive to the bonds that hold the couple together
   b) can be beneficial to a marital relationship
   c) is a predictor of marital distress
   d) has always been recommended by marriage counselors

3. Which theory holds that social communication is accomplished through the use of symbols:
   a) exchange theory
   b) conflict theory
   c) symbolic interaction theory
   d) structural functional theory

4. Which theory holds that commitment to a relationship is most likely to grow out of the relationship benefits:
   a) exchange theory
   b) conflict theory
   c) symbolic interactionism
   d) structural functional theory

5. Which theory holds that communication is often used to influence or dominate another person:
   a) exchange theory
   b) conflict theory
   c) symbolic interaction theory
   d) structural functional theory

6. Children who possess "perspective-taking skills" are much more likely than children who do not:
   a) to get their way with their parents
   b) to win arguments with their peers
   c) to be sought out as friends
   d) to engage in conflict with their peers

7. Mothers who use reflective listening with children tend to have children that:
   a) have difficult times making decisions
   b) are empathetic
   c) are prone to conflict with their peers
   d) need to get their own way with their peers

8. According to conflict theory, people give in to partners who threaten or give orders because:
   a) they lack communication skills
   b) they feel it is the best way to get their partner to leave them alone
   c) they feel that the best way to make a marriage work is by compromising one's needs
   d) they lack resources that provide them with power in a relationship

9. In communicating with their husbands, wives who are "equal partners" are much more likely than wives in "traditional partnerships" to:
   a) use an assertive approach, stating directly what they want
   b) use indirect strategies, such as dropping hints and flattering
   c) pose direct verbal threats to their husbands
   d) be verbally abusive towards their husbands

10. According to symbolic interaction theory, the most common use of symbols is found in:
   a) language
   b) hand signals
   c) facial expressions
   d) body language

11. It is important to understand the role of language in communication because all of the following except:
   a) language can alter our thoughts, attitudes, and concepts of reality
   b) language is our way of depicting absolute truths and our anchor to objective reality
   c) language can serve as an important source of people's self-concepts
   d) language is our most important and most commonly used symbol

12. Which of the following social theorists are best known for their theories about the development of the self?
   a) George Herbert Mead and Charles Horton Cooley
   b) Karl Marx and Emile Durkheim
   c) Lewis Coser and C. Wright Mills
   d) Max Weber and Robert Merton

13. According to social theorists, our identity:
 a) is something that develops through social interaction
 b) is something that we are born with
 c) is something that is bestowed upon us
 d) is usually set by the time we reach twelve years of age

14. Gunnysacking tends to be the result of which communication style?
 a) assertion
 b) non-assertion
 c) aggression
 d) non-aggression

15. When a person erupts in irritation over a last-straw trivial incident, it is likely to be the result of:
 a) the assumption of mind reading
 b) allowing the partner to define the situation
 c) gunnysacking
 d) aggressive communication

16. A partner is most likely to define the situation as one in which the other partner is to blame when which of the following communication styles is used?
 a) aggressive communication
 b) non-aggressive communication
 c) assertion
 d) non-assertion

17. Which type of communication style tends to be the most demeaning to the other partner?
 a) aggressive communication
 b) non-aggressive communication
 c) assertion
 d) non-assertion

18. Which communication style tends to be the most effective in resolving conflicts in marriage?
 a) aggressive communication
 b) non-aggressive communication
 c) assertion
 d) non-assertion

19. An expression of empathy is an example of:
   a) a bonding statement
   b) an "I"-statement
   c) concluding an assertive statement
   d) sympathy

20. People tend to take responsibility for their feelings and "own their feelings" when they:
   a) make bonding statements
   b) make "I"-statements
   c) express sympathy
   d) conclude an assertive statement

21. Asking for what you want is usually most effective when:
   a) it is part of the bonding statement
   b) it is part of the "I"-statements
   c) it occurs as part of the conclusion to an assertive statement
   d) it occurs indirectly so it does not give the appearance that you are being to aggressive

22. Which part of the assertive statement is most likely to change a whining statement into a powerful statement:
   a) the bonding statement
   b) "I"-statements
   c) the conclusion
   d) the aggressive statement

23. When Vuchinich studied family conversations at their dinner tables he found that family conflicts are most likely to be initiated:
   a) by the mother
   b) by the father
   c) by the children
   d) equally

24. Invalidation is a communication problem because:
   a) it violates a mate's right to be treated with respect
   b) it involves indirect messages in an effort to control the partner's behavior
   c) it leaves the message open to many interpretations
   d) it sends contradictory messages to the partner

25. An attempt to convince a partner that his or her feelings should not exist is a form of which communication problem?
a) invalidation
b) manipulation
c) indirect communication
d) double messages

NOTES:

PROJECTS

PROJECT 13. 1 Using Theories to Examine Communication in Your Family or Intimate Relationships

Each of the projects in this chapter ask you to examine communication in your family or personal relationships in one way or another. In this first project, you will look at communication in your family or other intimate relationship from the point of view of three sociological perspectives: exchange theory, conflict theory, and symbolic interactionism. The objectives of this activity are to teach you to gain more understanding of the various dynamics of communication in personal relationships, to provide you with practice in doing qualitative field research, and to give you practice doing a content analysis of your research.

Journal instructions:

1. Re-read the sections in Chapter 13 that discuss exchange, conflict, and symbolic interaction theories of communication. In your journal, summarize the main arguments of each theory, list and briefly explain the types of communication that each theory tends to look for in family communication (for example, exchange theory focuses on expressions of empathy, appreciation, and reflective listening), and discuss how each of these types of communication affects the relationship, according to the theory. Take your time with this instruction. Read the material very carefully. The types of communication that each theory would focus on do not necessarily appear in the section as key terms, so you will have to read the section carefully to determine this.

2. For one week, observe communication within your family: between parents, between parents and children, between children. Keep an extensive record in your journal of what you observe. Look for examples of the types of communication that you listed and discussed above. Try to include as much of the conversation as possible that enables you to determine the type of communication that is being used for each interaction. Sometimes the communication will occur so quickly that you will have to take some time after it is over and reflect in your journal about what had just happened and the type of communication that occurred.

3. After you have recorded your observations for one week, do a content analysis of your field work journal. What that means is that you will organize your observations into categories. In this case, the categories will be types of communication that you observed. Here is one way to proceed. As you read through your field work journal, write in the margin next to each example of communication that you observed the type of communication that it is. Was it an expression of empathy, appreciation, a threat, an interruption, a verbal or non-verbal symbol that affects self-concept, or other type of communication that you discussed in instruction #1? Or you may develop some other type of coding system to help you organize your journal notes.

4. When you complete your content analysis, write a brief conclusion in which you discuss which theory offers the best explanation of the dynamics of communication in your family. Select **only one** theory (even though each may offer good explanations) and explain your choice.

Option: essay

If you have not already done so, complete the above journal instructions. Write an essay (around four to five pages, typed) in which you examine and discuss communication in **your family** from the point of view of **each** of the theoretical perspectives on communication discussed in Chapter 13 (exchange theory, conflict theory, and symbolic interaction theory). Be sure to provide examples in your discussion. In the conclusion to your essay, discuss which theory you think offers the most accurate explanation of the dynamics of communication in your family.

Option: bibliography

Using your library's *Social Science Index* and other bibliographic indexes, develop a bibliography of ten to fifteen articles and/or books dealing with theories of communication in families. Be sure that at least half of your selections are from social science journals. Type your bibliography using the format in the journal articles or textbook.

Option: research paper

If you have not already done so, complete the journal instructions for this project. Write a paper (around eight to ten pages, typed) in which you use at least five items in your bibliography (above) to discuss your observations of communication in your family. There are a number of ways to conduct your analysis. For example, you may use information found in the bibliographic material to explain or discuss communication that you observed in your family. Or you may use your observations as examples of ideas that you read about in your bibliographic material. Another possibility would be to combine both of these approaches.

Examine your material and conduct an analysis in whichever way you feel is most appropriate to demonstrate your knowledge of the material. Be sure to document all of your bibliographic sources throughout your paper and include a works cited (reference) page.

NOTES:

PROJECT 13.2 Observing Communication Styles in Families or Intimate Groups

Like Project 13.1, this project involves observing communication in families. However, in this project you will observe and styles of communication. The objectives of this activity are to sensitize you to the various communications styles used in families and their degree of effectiveness and to enable you to develop further your field work research skills.

Journal instructions:

1. Re-read the section in Chapter 13 that discusses communication styles (non-assertion,aggression, and assertion) and components of an assertive statement. In your journal, summarize these styles of communication. Pay particular attention to Tables 13.1 and 13.2.

2. For one week, observe the styles of communication that are used in your family, another family that you have access to observing, or the group of people with whom you live. At various times during each day, write down descriptions of the interactions that are occuring among the group you are observing (including yourself), examples of the styles of communication that are being displayed, and the outcome of the interaction.

Suggestion: Before you begin your observations, you might want to develop a system that makes identifying and recording your observations easier. For example, look at the descriptions of the communication styles in Table 13.1. Each row seems to deal with a different category. The first row deals with how feelings are communicated. The second row deals with how direct the communication is. The third row deals with the extent to which one makes one's own choices. And so on. You might consider creating a "coding" sheet in which you list each category (how feelings are communicated, how direct communication is, and so on) and assign a number or a "code" to represent each one. Then, when you are making your observations, you can simply write down the code that represents what is occuring followed with an example from the situation. That will save you an enormous amount of recording time and allow you to obtain much more information. You can do something similar with the components of an empathetic statement as found in Table 13.2. You do not necessarily have to follow this approach. You should develop a system that you are comfortable with and that enables you to obtain as much accurate information as possible when you are doing your observations. Making preparations to record your observations as efficiently and as accurately as possible is a very important step in doing field work. It is suggested, therefore, that you take your time with this stage. It will affect the outcome of your research.

3. After you complete your week of observation, examine what you have recorded in terms of the categories that you developed when you prepared your journal for your observations. Discuss any patterns that you notice. For example, which are the most common styles of communication used? Do any methods tend to be more effective in providing successful communication or poor communication than others? Do certain people tend to use certain styles of communication? Do people tend to use the components of assertive statements that are discussed in the chapter? And so on.

Option: essay
Write an essay (around five pages, typed) in which you discuss communication styles in the family or group that you observed for one week. In your discussion, discuss things such as how you prepared your journal, when you made your observations, for how long, how you recorded your observations, any problems that you had in recording your observations, examples of the different categories on which the styles of communication are based, the types of communication styles that seemed most effective, who was most likely to use each type, and so on.

Option: bibliography
Use your library's *Social Science Index* and/or other indexes to develop a bibliography of ten to fifteen articles and/or books that deal with styles of communication in personal relationships. Make sure that at least ten of your selections are from social science journals or are books written by social scientists. Type your bibliography using the format in your textbook or in the social science journals.

Option: research paper
If you have not already done so, complete the journal instructions for this project. Write a paper (around eight to ten pages, typed) in which you use at least five items in your bibliography to discuss your observations of styles of communication in your family or in the group you observed. There are a number of ways to conduct your analysis. For example, you may use information found in the bibliographic material to explain or discuss communication that you observed in your family. Or you may use your observations as examples of ideas that you read about in your bibliographic material. Another possibility would be to combine both of these approaches. Examine your material and conduct an analysis in whichever way you feel is most appropriate to demonstrate your knowledge of the material. Be sure to document all of your bibliographic sources throughout your paper and include a works cited (reference) page.

NOTES:

PROJECT 13.3 Examining Conflict and Communication Problems

A section of Chapter 13 discusses a study by Vuchinich in which he examined family conflict by observing dinner-table conversations. In this activity you will follow Vuchinich's model and study dinner-table conversations in your family. The objectives of this activity are to help you understand how conflict is initiated in families, methods for stopping it, and the sources of communication problems and to provide you with more experience in conducting field work.

Journal instructions:

1. Re-read the sections in Chapter 13 about conflict and family roles and communication problems. In your journal, summarize the methods of stopping conflict that Vuchinich observed and the four types of communication problems.

2. Using Vuchinich's study as a model, for one week observe dinner-table conversations (and other conversations) in your family. In your journal keep a detailed record of who initiates conflicts, the methods used for stopping conflicts, and the communication problems (identified in Chapter 13) that exist. Fully describe each situation and provide rich detail as to what is said and what occurs.

3. At the end of the week, compare the results of your observations with Vuchinich's conclusions and the other conclusions about conflict and communication problems that Wolf discusses in Chapter 13. Discuss this in your journal.

Option: essay

Write an essay (around four to five pages, typed) in which you use your journal observations to discuss conflict and family roles and communication problems. Be sure to illustrate your discussion with examples from your journal. In addition, compare the results of your observations of conflict, family roles, and communication problems with the conclusions discussed by Wolf.

Option: bibliography

Develop a bibliography of ten to fifteen articles from social science journals and/or books written by social scientists about conflict and communication problems in families. Type your bibliography following the format found in the social science journals or in your textbook.

Option: research paper

If you have not already done so, complete the journal instructions for this project. Write a paper (around eight to ten pages, typed) in which you use at least five items in your bibliography (above) to discuss your observations of conflict and communication problems in your family. There are a number of ways to conduct your analysis. For example, you may use information found in the bibliographic material to explain or discuss the conflict and/or communication problems that you observed in your family. Or you may use your observations as examples of ideas that you read about in your bibliographic material. Another possibility would be to combine both of these approaches. Examine your material and conduct an analysis in whichever way you feel is most appropriate to demonstrate your knowledge of the material. Be sure to document all of your bibliographic sources throughout your paper and include a works cited (reference) page.

NOTES:

CHAPTER 14

FAMILY ABUSE AND VIOLENCE

CHAPTER OUTLINE

Battered Women
- Courtship Violence
- The Cycle of Violence
- Normalizing Violence

Battered Men

Explanations for Domestic Violence
- Psychological Explanations
- Conflict theory
- Exchange Theory
- Gender Role Theory

Factors Associated with Domestic Violence
- Substance Abuse
- Violent Childhood
- Social Class
- Race
- Status Differential
- Unemployment

Mitigating Domestic Violence
- Shelters
- Police-Initiated Arrests

Elder Abuse
- Dependency
- Social Isolation
- The Intergenerational Transmission of Violence
- Legal Guardianship

Sibling Abuse
- Age
- Gender
- Generalized Family Violence

Child Physical Abuse
- The Intergenerational Transmission of Violence
- The Effect of Violence on Boys
- The Effect of Violence on Girls

Child Sexual Abuse
- Effect on the Victim
- The Role of the Mother
- The Victim Precipitation Argument Examined

CHAPTER LEARNING OBJECTIVES

After studying this chapter, you should be able to:

• discuss patterns of courtship violence against women and how courtship violence is related to escalation of violence after marriage;

• identify and discuss the stages in a cycle of violence;

• discuss the extent to which violence against husbands is likely to occur;

• discuss and critique psychological explanations, conflict theory, exchange theory, and gender role theory as explanations for domestic violence;

• identify and discuss factors associated with domestic violence;

• identify and discuss factors that can reduce the amount of domestic violence and make it easier for battered women to leave a violent relationship;

• discuss the factors associated with the likelihood of elder abuse;

• discuss the extent to which sibling abuse occurs and factors related to it;

• discuss the extent to which child abuse occurs, reasons for its occurrence, and its effects on children;

• discuss the extent to which child sexual abuse occurs, the factors which precipitate it, and its long-term effects on children.

KEY POINTS FOR REVIEW

• One-fifth of female college students report that they have been victims of physical force—such as pushing or shoving—on a date. Four percent had actually been battered by clenched fists. Low self-esteem on the part of the victim, a belief that the violent partner will change, and fear of retaliation make it difficult for many women to escape violent dating relationships. Although physical assaults that occur in a relationship prior to marriage are typically mild, these types of assaults tend to escalate into more severe physical violence after marriage.

• The battering of women usually follows a pattern known as the cycle of violence. This cycle typically has three stages: tension building, the violent incident, and contrition and courtship. Violence in a relationship tends to become normalized when the violent partner no longer defines the violent behavior as deviant.

• Although violence against husbands appears to have occurred almost as often as against wives, the statistics can be misleading because of the types of questions asked. Women typically endure the worst in violent relationships.

• Four major explanations for domestic violence include psychological explanations, conflict theory, exchange theory, and gender role theory. Psychological explanations focus on mental process within the violent individual such as lack of impulse control, paranoia, the Dr. Jekyll and Mr. Hyde syndrome, and emotional dependence on the battered victim. An important criticism of this theory is that the typical batterer is usually not out of control or acting solely on impulse during the violent episode.

• Conflict theory argues that violence is used as a means to gain power in a relationship. Violence is much more likely to occur in male-dominant relationships than in egalitarian relationships and is often the means through which the male maintains his position of dominance. A criticism of conflict theory is that it does not account for violence in egalitarian relationships.

• Exchange theory maintains that people are rational and will continue to be violent as long as the rewards outweigh the costs. This theory also helps to explain why a battered person may remain with an abuser. Criticisms of this theory are that resources, costs, and rewards are difficult to measure in a relationship and that people do not necessarily make rational choices.

• Gender role theory explains violence in a relationship is rooted in traditional gender roles. A battered woman who adheres to traditional gender roles may put the needs for her partner's forgiveness above her own safety and also feel that it is her responsibility to solve the problem. An abusive husband who adheres to traditional gender roles often believes that he has the right to determine the rules for his wife and often explains his violence as a reaction to his wife's failure to obey his rules. A criticism of this theory is that it does not explain why some men alter their traditional gender behavior to fit new circumstances, nor does it explain all forms of family violence.

• Factors that have been associated with domestic violence include substance abuse, a violent childhood, social class, race, status differential between the partners, and unemployment. Although domestic violence occurs in all social classes, it tends to occur more often in lower income families. Domestic violence occurs more often among African-Americans, but this is likely because African-Americans are over-represented among the poor.

• Two factors that are important in mitigating or reducing the amount of domestic violence and make it easier for battered women to leave a violent relationship are battered women's shelters and police-initiated arrests of violent partners.

• Studies estimate that approximately 4 percent of elderly persons have been physically, emotionally, or financially abused by a relative, but this may be an underestimate. Factors associated with the likelihood of elder abuse include the dependency of the elder parent on the adult child for care, the degree of social isolation of the elderly person, and whether or not the adult child had been the victim of abuse.

• The most common type of family violence is sibling abuse. Americans tend to be tolerant of sibling abuse, often dismissing it as being natural for one child to hit another. Sibling abuse tends to occur more often by preschool children, boys, and in families that are plagued by violence.

• Over 2 million children are physically abused or neglected each year. Children can be exposed to violence both as targets and as observers. Children who are exposed to violence are at a higher risk for the intergenerational transmission of violence. This occurs as children learn through their role models. Physically abused children tend to have emotional problems, such as low self-esteem, and tend to become involved with substance abuse.

• Child sexual abuse is widespread. Effects of child sexual molestation for children include role confusion for the child, confusion, depression, crying, shame, and guilt. In addition, it may lead to the lack of trust and affection toward others, and chemical dependency as adults.

• For many years, explanations of child sexual abuse rested on the victim precipitation argument which claims that the child initiates the sexual abuse. This view failed to take into account the cultural expectation of obedience to parental demands and, thus, blames the victim. Recently, new directions in sex education teach children to demand that sexual abuse stop and to tell a responsible adult when they suspect that is occurring.

KEY TERMS

The following key terms are found in your textbook on the page number indicated in parentheses. In the space provided, write a brief definition of the key term. Then provide an example of the term, such as a culture in which the practice takes place, or people that you might know whose behavior illustrates the term. You could include issues that you might have read about in the news or in a book, or anything else that will illustrate the term and help you remember it. Include any comments from your class discussions or textbook that might help you remember and understand these key terms.

violence (p. 383)

____

____

____

cycle of violence (p. 384)

____

____

____

tension building (p. 384)

____

____

____

trigger incident (p. 384)

____

____

contrition (p. 385)

paranoia (p. 388)

Dr. Jekyll and Mr. Hyde syndrome (p. 388)

psychological theories (p. 387)

conflict theory (p. 389)

exchange theory (p. 390)

gender role theory (p. 391)

status differential (p. 395)

role model (p. 400)

intergenerational transmission of violence (p. 400)

learned helplessness (p. 402)

sexual abuse (p. 402)

role confusion (p. 402)

victim precipitation (p. 404)

NOTES:

PRACTICE TEST

Multiple Choice

1. When physical force occurs in dating relationships, it is usually in the form of:
   a) date rape
   b) pushing and shoving
   c) hitting with clenched fists
   d) women protecting themselves against men

2. All of the following are reasons that make it difficult for many women to escape violent dating relationships except:
   a) low self-esteem on the part of the victim
   b) the psychological need for some women to be abused
   c) a belief that the violent partner will change
   d) fear that the violent partner will retaliate

3. When severe violence is present in a relationship, physical violence usually begins:
   a) early in the courtship period
   b) after steady dating with each other begins
   c) within the first five years of marriage
   d) after a couple has been married ten years

4. Hints of potential violence, such as excessive jealousy, attempting to control the partner's behavior, alcohol and drug abuse, and the expression of anger by hitting physical objects, are expressed:
   a) usually in the courtship period
   b) only after the couple is engaged
   c) usually not until a couple has become married
   d) usually after one of the married partners begins to become dissatisfied with the relationship

5. Which of the following is not considered by social scientists to be part of the cycle of violence?
   a) tension building
   b) provoking the violent partner
   c) the violent incident
   d) expressions of remorse and courtship

6. Twelve percent of husbands and 11 percent of wives used violence against their mates during a one-year period. Upon examination of the study that provided this statistic, social scientists found which of the following statements to be an accurate conclusion?
   a) husbands and wives are, for all practical purposes, equally violent
   b) there is a parity of violence in which physical fights in marriage are equally balanced
   c) violence against husbands is as prevalent a social issue as violence against wives
   d) the questionnaire that resulted in this statistic did not consider the actual number of physical assaults that took place in a marriage, or the extent of the injury to the victim

7. Which explanation for domestic violence maintains that people are likely to continue in their acts of violence as long as the benefits they receive as a result outweigh the costs of their violent behavior?
   a) psychological explanations
   b) conflict theory
   c) exchange theory
   d) gender role theory

8. Which explanation for domestic violence argues that women often stay in violent relationships because they feel that is their responsibility to work out the family's problems?
   a) psychological explanations
   b) conflict theory
   c) exchange theory
   d) gender role theory

9. Which explanation for domestic violence accounts for the abuser's behavior as a result of a lack of impulse control, paranoia, the Dr. Jekyll and Mr. Hyde syndrome, and an emotional dependence on the partner?
   a) psychological explanations
   b) conflict theory
   c) exchange theory
   d) gender role theory

10. Which explanation for domestic violence accounts for the violence as an attempt of the abuser to gain decision-making power and increase one's control of sexual property in the relationship?
   a) psychological explanations
   b) conflict theory
   c) exchange theory
   d) gender role theory

11. Which of the following statements characterizes the relationship between substance abuse and family violence?
a) ending the substance abuse usually leads to the end of violence
b) men who beat their wives when they are drunk are not likely to beat them when they are sober
c) violent partners usually resort to abusing alcohol or drugs as a substitute for battering their spouses
d) people who abuse their spouses often use alcohol or drugs before hand to avoid taking responsibility for their violent actions

12. Violence in the family is much more likely to occur:
a) among low-income families
b) among middle-income families
c) among upper-middle income families
d) among upper-income families

13. Domestic violence against women occurs more often in African-American families because:
a) African-Americans are socialized to be more accepting of violence and to use violence as a means of communication
b) African-Americans are more likely to embrace traditional gender roles than white Americans
c) African-Americans are more likely to be poor than white-Americans
d) there are more likely to be status differences between African-American husbands and wives

14. Of the factors listed below, which two are the most important in reducing domestic violence and making it easier for battered women to leave violent relationships?
a) teaching women how to disagree with their husbands and making women's shelters more available
b) police-initiated arrests of violent husbands and teaching women how to disagree with their husbands without provoking them
c) the increased availability of battered-women's shelters and police-initiated arrests
d) counseling for abusive husbands and teaching women how to disagree with their husbands without provoking them

15. Elder abuse is MOST likely to occur when:
a) the elderly parent becomes physically dependent on the adult child for care
b) the elderly parent is independent and expresses few needs from the adult child
c) when the perpetrators of elder abuse were themselves physically abused as children
d) when the elderly person is socially isolated

16. The extreme willingness of courts to assume that elderly persons are incompetent and to assign legal guardianship of the elderly person to a younger relative:
a) has proven to be a positive step in decreasing and controlling elder abuse in the United States
b) is usually warranted because of the increase in the life-span that has occurred in the past century
c) tends to provide more freedom and dignity to the elderly since they no longer have to worry about supporting themselves
d) tends to infantalize the elderly person and rob that person of the right to make decisions that affect his or her life

17. The most common form of family violence in the United States is:
a) elder abuse
b) wife abuse
c) husband abuse
d) sibling abuse

18. Which of the following is not generally associated with explaining levels of sibling abuse:
a) age
b) gender
c) extent of family violence
d) race

19. Children who are victims of violence and children who observe violence against other family members:
a) are less likely to become violent adults because of the damage they have seen as a result of it
b) generally overcome the effects of the violence they experienced and observed by the time they become parents themselves
c) are at a higher risk for becoming violent adults than children who are not exposed to violence
d) tend to be more nurturing parents than children who have never been exposed to violence

20. Which theory argues that intergenerational transmission of violence occurs through observation of family role models?
a) social learning theory
b) exchange theory
c) conflict theory
d) structural functional theory

21. By observing violence in the family, children tend to incorporate all of the following assumptions into their views of family life except:
a) violence is rewarded by compliance from the battered person
b) violence is considered an appropriate solution to family problems
c) people who love them are most likely to hurt them and physical force appears justified when something is really important
d) violence is harmful to the development of children and detrimental to family stability

22. One important factor that is most likely to mitigate against the long-term negative effects of a violent childhood is:
a) the presence of another sibling who has also been abused
b) the presence of a nurturing parent in the home
c) placing the child in a foster home
d) religious training for the child

23. An explanation of child sexual abuse that is no longer accepted by social scientists is:
a) the victim precipitation argument
b) role confusion
c) social learning theory
d) gender role theory

24. Children who are sexually abused are much more likely to:
a) develop close, intimate relationships in adulthood
b) be better lovers with their spouses
c) have a lack of trust in adult relationships
d) have a lack of sexual desire in adult relationships

25. Freud's explanation of victimized children's willingness to give in to the sexual demands of a relative and their willingness to keep it a secret was that:
a) children were living up to the cultural norms of obedience to parents
b) children secretly fantasize about having sexual relations with the opposite-sex parent
c) children are unaware of the difference between right and wrong
d) children suffer from a role confusion that inhibits their abilities to know exactly what is required of them

NOTES:

PROJECTS

PROJECT 14. 1 Observing Abuse and Family Violence

As Robin Wolf discusses in Chapter 14, family violence and violence in intimate relationships—including battered women, battered men, child abuse, child molestation, elder abuse, and sibling abuse—are widespread social problems. The objectives of this project are to sensitize you to the extent to which family abuse occurs, to have you examine family abuse in terms of the explanations and factors discussed in Chapter 14, and (if you do the research paper) to compare how family abuse/violence is discussed in social science journals and in news reports.

Journal instructions:

1. Use your library's indexes to locate around twenty newspaper and news magazine articles that have reported about various forms of family abuse and violence either nationally and/or in the area where you live for the past year.

2. For each article:
   a) Indicate the type of abuse or violence that each article describes (battered women, battered men, child abuse, elder abuse, sibling abuse, or child molestation).
   b) Make a list of the factors associated with the abuse or violence in each situation. Use Wolf's discussion on factors associated with domestic violence as a guide to help you identify the factors in each situation. However, if there are factors other than the one's Wolf discusses, include them in your list.

3. Use the information in each article to explain as best you can the reasons for the abuse/violence from the point of view of psychological explanations, conflict theory, exchange theory, or gender role theory. Find evidence in the articles to support one or more of these explanations for domestic violence, as discussed by Wolf in Chapter 14.

4. Summarize the factors associated with the abuse or violence that you read about in the articles. For example, what percentage of situations involved alcohol and/or other drugs? What percentage of cases involved a person who grew up in a violent family? And so on.

5. Summarize your conclusions about the explanations for domestic violence that you were able to find evidence for from the articles.

Option: essay

Using the information and analysis from your observations (above) write an essay (around five pages, typed) in which you discuss factors associated with domestic violence and explanations for domestic violence in the area and during the time period about which you conducted your research.

Option: bibliography
Use the *Social Science Index* or other library indexes of social science journals to develop a bibliography of fifteen articles from social science journals about family abuse and/or violence. Type your bibliography using proper bibliographic style.

Option: research paper
Write a paper (around seven to nine pages, typed) in which you use material from four or five articles from you bibliography to discuss the results of your analysis of news reports of family abuse/violence. Some things to include in your discussion may be:

a) Compare how social science journals and news reports discuss violence and abuse;

b) Apply some of the ideas found in the social science journals to the results of your analysis. For example, are their any theories, explanations, or conclusions discussed in the social science journal articles that you can use to explain the cases that you observed in the news reports?

c) Use examples or conclusions from your observations of news reports to illustrate the ideas or conclusions found in the social science journals.

Provide proper documentation of your references throughout your paper and include a reference page.

CHAPTER 15

DIVORCE

CHAPTER OUTLINE

Trends
- Explanation for the 1965 to 1980 Divorce Boom
- No-Fault Divorce

Who Runs the Highest Risk of Divorce?
- Age at First Marriage
- Education
- Presence of Children
- Premarital Birth
- Socioeconomic Status
- Parent's Marital History
- Race

Why Do People Divorce?
- Sexual Dissatisfaction and Extramarital Affairs
- Drifting Apart
- Substance Abuse and Domestic Violence
- Economic Crisis

Divorce Theories
- Exchange Theory
- Conflict Theory

The Financial Impact of Divorce
- The Financial Position of Custodial Parents
- Child Support
- Divorced Parents and Poverty
- Displaced Homemakers

Emotional Adjustment to Divorce
- Stages of Adjustment to Divorce
- Relationship with the Former Spouse

Children's Post-Divorce Adjustment

- Short-Term Difficulties
- Long-Term Consequences
- Economic and Social Disruption
- Impaired Parenting Ability
- Critique of the "Divorce Damages Children" Position

Parental Conflict After Divorce

- Continuing Parental Conflict
- Triangulation

Child Custody

The Non-Custodial Parent

- How Often Do Non-Resident Fathers See Their Children?
- Which Divorced Fathers Stay in Touch?
- Non-Custodial Mothers

CHAPTER LEARNING OBJECTIVES

After studying this chapter, you should be able to:

- discuss divorce trends in the United States and reasons for the dramatic rise in divorce from the 1960s to the 1980s;

- discuss who runs the highest risk of divorce and explain why;

- identify and discuss the reasons why people divorce;

- discuss exchange theory and conflict theory as they apply to divorce and the period following a divorce;

- discuss the financial impact of divorce on parents and children;

- identify and discuss the emotional stages that people go through after divorce;

- identify and discuss the short-term and long-term difficulties faced by children of divorce;

- discuss the effects of parental conflict after divorce on children;

- identify and discuss the different forms of child custody;

- discuss the relationship between the non-custodial parent and the child.

KEY POINTS FOR REVIEW

- There was a dramatic rise in the divorce rate in the United States between 1960 and 1980. Explanations for the rapid rise in divorce during this period include growing marital dissatisfaction, the declining wages of men, the employment of married women, extended life expectancy, decline in social support for marriage, and the "no-fault" divorce system.

- The "no-fault divorce system" is one in which couples can divorce on the basis of incompatibility and neither partner is assumed to have caused the divorce. This is in contrast to the adversarial divorce system in which one person had to prove that the other committed adultery, cruelty, or some other wrong-doing.

• The risk of divorce is affected by age at first marriage, education, the presence of children, a prior non-marital birth, parents' marital history, socioeconomic status, and race. The single most important factor influencing the risk of divorce is age at marriage.

• The factors that often precipitate divorce include sexual dissatisfaction, extramarital affairs, drifting apart, substance abuse, domestic violence, and economic problems.

• Exchange theory examines divorce in terms of the rewards and costs it provides to the couple. From this point of view, people are less likely to get divorced the longer they have been married because the costs of marital break-up increase and the benefits of being single decrease as the duration of marriage increases. Conflict theory examines divorce by looking at how the distribution of resources affects the well-being of family members after divorce.

• While the income of both men and women declines after divorce, the decline in standard of living tends to be particularly severe for custodial mothers. One important reason for this is the increase in the no-fault divorce system. As a result, the deteriorating economic position of children after divorce has become a serious national issue. The "feminization of poverty" refers to the situation in which an increasing number of women and children are experiencing impoverishment after divorce. Although not as widespread, there are many impoverished custodial fathers also.

• People generally go through a series of stages as they adjust to divorce. The acute stage—which lasts from one to two years—is a period of emotional upheaval characterized by anger, depression, and loneliness. In the transition stage most people come to terms with the divorce and accept their new life as a single person. During the restabilization stage—which generally begins three to five years after separation—people finally establish an identity separate from a relationship with a former spouse.

• After a divorce, children may experience both short-term and long-term negative consequences. Short term consequences are likely to include problems related to emotional and physical functioning and academic problems. Long-term consequences include the greater likelihood of experiencing a divorce in their own marriage as adults and a higher rate of out-of-wedlock births to teens from divorced families.

• Recent research indicates that it may not be the divorce itself that has the negative impact on the children but the economic and social disruption and impaired parenting ability that is associated with divorce. Divorce does not necessarily have a negative impact on children. In some cases it may even result in positive consequences for children.

• A major factor associated with distress in children after divorce is ongoing parental conflict following the divorce. Children whose parents get along well after the divorce tend to be better adjusted than children whose parents continue to engage in conflict.

• Whereas in the past most divorce cases resulted in sole custody of children, all states now offer the option of joint custody. In joint legal custody the parents share decision-making authority. In joint physical custody, the children actually have two residences. Joint custody is advantageous for children when the parents are able to get along.

• Over half of the children of divorce have no contact with the non-custodial parent. Contact with the non-custodial parent tends to decline with time after separation. Factors that affect the amount of contact fathers have with their children following divorce include the socioeconomic status of the father, the marital status of both parents, and the age and gender of children. While non-custodial mothers tend to stay in contact with their children, there is currently little information about the factors that affect their amount of contact.

NOTES:

KEY TERMS

The following key terms are found in your textbook on the page number indicated in parentheses. In the space provided, write a brief definition of the key term. Then provide an example of the term, such as a culture in which the practice takes place, or people that you might know whose behavior illustrates the term. You could include issues that you might have read about in the news or in a book, or anything else that will illustrate the term and help you remember it. Include any comments from your class discussions or textbook that might help you remember and understand these key terms.

no-fault divorce (p. 416)

____

____

____

adversarial divorce (p. 415)

____

____

____

sex-ratio imbalance (p. 420)

____

____

____

exchange theory (p. 423)

____

____

conflict theory (p. 423)

principle of equity (p. 417)

assumption of self-sufficiency (p. 425)

standard of living (p. 424)

displaced homemaker (p. 427)

preoccupation (p. 428)

sleeper effect for girls (p. 431)

self-absorption (p. 432)

triangulation (p. 434)

joint physical custody (p. 434)

joint legal custody (p. 434)

____

____

____

NOTES:

PRACTICE TEST

Multiple Choice

1. Between the early 1960s and 1980s, the divorce rate in the United States:
   a) remained about the same
   b) doubled
   c) tripled
   d) decreased by around half

2. According to demographers, approximately how many people who enter marriage this decade will eventually divorce?
   a) 25 percent
   b) 33 percent
   c) 50 percent
   d) 66 percent

3. Which of the following has not been found to be an explanation for the increase in the divorce rate during the late 1960s and 1970s?
   a) a decline in the value placed on the family
   b) marital dissatisfaction
   c) the declining wages of men
   d) extended life expectancy

4. The employment of married women has tended to:
   a) create more stable marriages
   b) increase the level of agreement between husbands and wives
   c) promote divorce
   d) increase the level of quality time parents provide to children

5. A "no-fault divorce system" means that:
   a) if no fault is proven to exist on the part of one of the partners, no divorce is granted
   b) the new system of divorce in the United States is much improved over systems of the past
   c) neither person is assumed to be at fault in causing the divorce
   d) it is more difficult for persons who have been divorced to re-marry each other

6. Of the following, who is most likely to experience a divorce?
   a) a couple that marries in their mid- to late-twenties and has children
   b) a couple that marries in their teens and does not have children
   c) a couple that marries in their teens and has children
   d) an upper-middle class couple that has graduated from college and marries in their twenties

7. The single most important factor influencing the risk of divorce is:
   a) age at marriage
   b) the presence of children
   c) parent's marital history
   d) socioeconomic status

8. That African Americans have a higher divorce rate than whites is most likely due to the fact that:
   a) African Americans traditionally have placed less value on the nuclear family than whites
   b) African-American men tend to be more promiscuous than white men
   c) African Americans face a sex-ratio imbalance that encourages divorce
   d) it is easier for African Americans to obtain a divorce than for whites

9. The sex-ratio imbalance that African Americans face means that:
   a) African Americans have a higher rate of adultery than whites
   b) there are a larger number of unattached African American women than unattached African American men
   c) there are a larger number of unattached African American men than unattached African American women
   d) African American men tend to want to value a sexual relationship more than African American women do

10. The most often-given reason by divorced couples for their marriage breaking up is:
   a) infidelity
   b) drifting apart
   c) substance abuse
   d) economic crisis

11. Which theory focuses on the distribution of resources among husbands and wives after a divorce?
   a) exchange theory
   b) conflict theory
   c) symbolic interaction theory
   d) structural functional theory

12. According to exchange theory, which of the following is most likely to be true?
a) the longer a couple is married, the greater the costs of marital break-up and the lower the benefits of being single
b) the longer a couple is married, the greater the costs of staying together and the greater the benefits of being single
c) men tend to have more discretionary income to spend on recreation, food, and clothing than women after a divorce
d) women tend to have greater resources after a divorce because of the alimony and child-support usually awarded to them

13. The assumption of self-sufficiency that underlies the "no-fault divorce system" has generally resulted in:
a) fewer economic hardships for women and children
b) fewer economic hardships for custodial fathers
c) greater economic hardships for non-custodial fathers
d) greater economic hardships for custodial women and their children

14. The "feminization of poverty" refers to:
a) the belief that impoverished men are poor because of their failure to live up to a traditional masculine gender role
b) the belief that poverty strips a man of his pride and, as a result, of his traditional role in the family
c) the growing impoverishment of single women and children
d) the view that poverty is considered as socially unacceptable as it once was

15. The first stage that people typically experience after separation is the:
a) acute stage
b) transition stage
c) debilitization stage
d) restabilization stage

16. Generally, how long does it take for a person to establish an identity separate from a relationship with the former spouse after separation:
a) around six months to a year
b) around one to two years
c) around three to five years
d) around six to eight years

17. What percentage of American children can expect to spend some time in a one-parent home before they reach age 18?
a) 10 percent
b) 25 percent
c) 50 percent
d) 75 percent

18. Which of the following are children of divorce likely to experience as short-term problems?
a) emotional problems
b) physical problems
c) academic problems
d) all of the above

19. The "sleeper effect," related to problem children of divorce experience, shows up most among:
a) teenage girls
b) teenage boys
c) adult men
d) adult women

20. Which of the following statements about the effects of divorce on children is least likely to be true?
a) Parental divorce can actually have a positive influence on children.
b) Parental divorce often has long term consequences for children.
c) Divorce itself does not lead to problems for children but, rather, the economic and social disruption that often accompanies divorce.
d) Parental divorce is always accompanied by emotional, physical, and academic problems for young children.

21. Social scientists tend to see divorce as:
a) one event in a long conflict process that began much before the divorce occurred
b) the outcome of a marriage suddenly beset by unsurmountable problems
c) an indication of a couple's values surrounding the family
d) the ultimate destruction of the family

22. Social scientists have found generally that parents who experience high levels of conflict during marriage tend to:
a) have much less conflict after divorce than parents who did not air their differences during marriage
b) continue to have conflict-ridden relationships for at least a year after divorce
c) ignore one another after divorce
d) develop a close friendship with one another after divorce

23. A study of divorced parents found that one year after divorce, mothers who were in conflict with their former spouses were characterized by all of the following except:
a) less warmth and less empathy than mother-child relationships in divorced families where former spouses got along well
b) less ego control, such as the inability to control outbursts of temper
c) lower expectations for ego control in their children
d) lower expectations for their children's academic achievement

24. When parents divorce, joint physical custody of the children:
a) is always advantageous to the children, whether or not both parents request it
b) is rapidly becoming the standard type of custody and currently takes place in over half of all custody settlements
c) is usually advantageous to children only when both parents request it
d) is disadvantageous for children, regardless of whether parents want it

25. Which of the following factors is least likely to affect the amount of contact that non-custodial fathers have with their children after a divorce:
a) socioeconomic status of the father
b) marital status of both parents
c) the age and gender of the children
d) the religious beliefs of the father

NOTES:

PROJECTS

PROJECT 15. 1 Who Runs the Highest Risk of Divorce?

In a section in Chapter 15, Robin Wolf explains that not everyone is at the same risk of divorce. Clearly, there are social variables related to the level of risk—age at marriage, education, presence of children, premarital birth, socioeconomic status, parents' marital history, and race. The objectives of this project are to have you gain some experience in conducting a survey and to have you gain a better understanding of what leads to divorce.

Journal instructions:

1. This survey can be conducted alone or with a group of students. Locate a sample of around one hundred students from your school that you can use to complete the survey found on pages 253 and 254 of this study guide. For the purposes of this project it might be easiest to use a "convenience sample" consisting of one or more classes at your college. Obtain permission from the appropriate professors before distributing the questionnaires to the classes.

2. If you do this survey with other members of your class, place the completed questionnaires in a location that you will each have access to.

3. Your objective is to determine what variables (factors) help to explain whether or not people are likely to get divorced. If you are analyzing your results by computer, cross-tabulate question number #1 with each of the other questions. If you are doing your analysis by hand, proceed as follows.

a) Separate the questionnaires into two piles based on question #1: divorced parents and not divorced parents.
b) For each pile, determine the number of responses given to each possible response for each question. For example, for question #2 indicate how many people said 0 - 1 year, how many people said 2 - 4 years, and so on.
c) Summarize your results for divorced and not divorced parents on two blank questionnaire forms. That is, use a questionnaire form to summarize the answers of people with divorced parents and another form to summarize the answers of people whose parents are not divorced.

Note: If you know how to perform computerized statistical analysis you can do so instead of performing the above analysis by hand. If you do a computerized analysis, obtain a frequency distribution of the questionnaire responses and then cross-tabulate question #1 with each of the other questions.

4. In your journal, discuss whether or not there are obvious differences in the responses related to divorced and not divorced parents. Compare your findings with the discussion of risk factors presented by Robin Wolf in Chapter 15.

5. In your journal, discuss which items on the questionnaire might be used if you were to explain divorce with exchange theory? For conflict theory?

Option: essay
Using the results of the above survey, write an essay (around five pages, typed) in which you discuss risk factors associated with divorce. In your essay, try to incorporate responses from the open-ended question #14 into your discussion of risk factors. Use responses to this question as examples or as explanations of some of the risk factors. Do the results of your survey lend themselves to either exchange theory or conflict theory? If so, discuss as part of your essay.

Option: bibliography
Develop a bibliography of ten articles from the *Reader's Guide to Periodical Literature* and ten articles from the *Social Science Index* within the past few years that contain discussions about the causes of divorce. Type your bibliography using the format found in your textbook or in one of the social science journal articles.

Option: research paper
Use material from four or five articles from you bibliography (at least two should be from social science journals) and your observations (above) to write a paper (around seven to nine pages, typed) in which you discuss factors associated with the risk of divorce. If you have already completed the above essay, you can use that as a first draft of your paper. Integrate your bibliographic sources into your essay. You can use them to help explain factors associated with risk, or you can use your survey results to help illustrate ideas found within the articles.

Provide proper documentation of your references throughout your paper and include a reference page.

NOTES:

"Risk of Divorce" Survey

INSTRUCTIONS:

This survey is being conducted for a class in marriage and the family. The purpose of the survey is to identify some of the factors that might increase or decrease the risk of separation and/or divorce.

Please answer the following questions about your parents as best as you can. The questions refer to your biological or adopted parents, not your stepparents. All questions refer to the most current time when your parents were married to each other. For example, age at marriage means age at marriage to **each other**. Highest education means highest education they had obtained **prior to or during their marriage to each other**, not after being separated or divorced. Education refers to the highest education they had obtained **as of the time they were married to each other** (not the highest level achieved after their separation). Income refers to most current level of income **while married to each other**. And so on.

1. Are your parents separated/divorced from each other? Yes____ No_____

2. How long have your parents been married or were married to each other?

Check one:

0 - 1 years _____
2 - 4 years _____
5 - 7 years _____
8 - 10 years _____
11 - 15 years _____
more than 15 years_____

3. Age at marriage?

Check one for each parent:

	mother	father
below 17	_____	_____
18 - 21	_____	_____
22 - 25	_____	_____
26 - 30	_____	_____
31 or above	_____	_____

4. Highest education completed

Check one for each parent:

	mother	father
elementary school	_____	_____
high school	_____	_____

college _____ _____
post-college education _____ _____
(graduate school, law school, _____ _____
medical school, etc)

5. Number of children _________

6. Did they have a premarital child? Yes_____ No_____ Don't know_____

7. Occupation

mother_____________________________

father______________________________

8. Income level (combined)

Check one:

under 15,000 _____
15,000 - 25,000_____
26,000 - 50,000_____
51,000-100,000_____
above 100,000 _____

9. Were either of your parents' parents divorced?

mother	Yes_____	No_____	Don't know_____
father	Yes_____	No_____	Don't know_____

10. Have either of your parents been divorced before marrying each other?

mother	Yes_____	No_____	Don't know_____
father	Yes_____	No_____	Don't know_____

11. Race

mother______________________

father______________________

12. Religion

mother______________________

father_______________________

12. Did they cohabit with each other before being married? Yes______ No______

If yes, how long?_______

14. If your parents are separated or divorced, what do **you** think led your parents to separate or divorce? Describe as best you can in your own words.

PROJECT 15. 2 Comparing Different Forms of Child Custody

There are a variety of forms of child custody after a divorce. There can be custodial-mothers, custodial fathers, joint legal custody, joint physical custody, and perhaps a few other variations that Robin Wolf does not mention. The objective of this project is to have you compare different forms of child custody especially with regard to what seems to work best for the children.

Journal instructions:
Form a group of around five people from your class and/or friends who come from families in which the parents divorced. Set aside about an hour to talk about the type of child custody arrangement that was developed. Keep detailed notes of the discussion in your journal. You can have a non-structured discussion or you can proceed as follows:

a) Go around the group and have each person introduce him or her self and briefly tell about the circumstances of the divorce (when it happened, how he or she was, any significant things that happened, and so on). The purpose of this step is to get the people in the group to know each other and to become comfortable with each other.

b) Go around the group a second time and have each person tell about the child custody arrangement. Did one parent have custody? Who? Was it joint custody? If so, was it joint legal custody or joint physical custody? Who was the primary custodian?

c) Go around the group a third time and have each person mention what he or she liked about the custody arrangement.

d) Go around the group a fourth time and have each person mention what he or she disliked about the arrangement.

e) Finally, ask each person in the group to provide some overall judgment about the type of custody that they experienced and how they would change it.

If possible, do the above with at least two or three different groups and keep a detailed record of the discussion within each group.

Option: essay
Using information you collected from your journal exercise above, and information from Robin Wolf's discussion of child custody in Chapter 15, write an essay (around five pages, typed) in which you compare different types of child custody.

Option: bibliography
Develop a bibliography of twenty articles from social science journals and popular periodicals and/or books written by social scientists that discuss types of child custody. Type the bibliography following the format found in the social science journals or in your textbook.

Option: research paper
Write a paper (around seven to nine pages, typed) in which you use information you collected from the research you did above and at least five items from your bibliography to discuss and compare different forms of child custody. Be sure that at least three items from your bibliography are articles from social science journal or books written by social scientists. Provide proper documentation throughout your paper and include a reference page.

NOTES:

CHAPTER 16

LOOKING FORWARD: EMERGING TRENDS AND FUTURE POTENTIALS

CHAPTER OUTLINE

Divorce and Co-Parenting in the Future
- Should Divorce Be More Difficult to Obtain?
- Post-Divorce Relationships
- Encouraging Fathering
- Regaining Confidence

Remarriage
- Factors that Affect Remarriage
- Cohabitation and Remarriage

Stepfamilies
- Incidence
- Stepfamilies with Residential Stepchildren
- Families with Visiting Stepchildren
- Characteristics of Stepfamilies
- Cohesion
- Adaptability
- Discipline in Stepfamilies
- The Age of Stepchildren

Redivorce
- Explanations for Redivorce
- African Americans and Redivorce
- Relationships with Stepchildren after Redivorce

AIDS and the Family
- Old and New AIDS Risk Groups
- Family Response to AIDS Victims
- Social Isolation and Discrimination

Unlaunched Adult Children
- Parental Reaction to Co-Residence
- Factors Promoting Adjustment to Co-Residence

Changing Families/Strengthening Families

Resilient Families
- Viewing Love as Multifaceted
- Keeping the Sexual Relationship Vital
- Spending Time Together
- Sharing Family Responsibilities
- Pregnancy as a Bonding Experience
- Authoritative Parenting
- Assertive Communication
- Non-violent Conflict Resolution
- Easing the Divorce Experience for Children

CHAPTER LEARNING OBJECTIVES

After studying this chapter, you should be able to:

- discuss reasons for and against making divorce more difficult to obtain;
- discuss factors that affect the likelihood and timing of remarriage;
- identify and discuss the four types of stepfamilies with residential stepchildren;
- identify and discuss two types of families with visiting stepchildren;
- identify and discuss the ways in which stepfamilies differ from traditional nuclear families;
- discuss three ways stepparents handle discipline issues;
- discuss the factors that influence the kind of relationship that develops between children and their stepparents;
- discuss the incidence of redivorce and two explanations for it;
- discuss the relationships between stepparents and their stepchildren after redivorce;
- identify and discuss the spread of AIDS among old and new AIDS risk groups;
- identify and discuss the stages that family members typically experience when a family member contracts AIDS;
- discuss parental reactions to co-residence with unlaunched children;
- identify and discuss three factors that promote adjustment to co-residence with unlaunched children;
- summarize the characteristics that social scientists have found enhance the rewards of family life.

KEY POINTS FOR REVIEW

• Recognizing that divorce is so widespread and that it frequently brings economic and emotional hardships to families, many social scientists are questioning whether or not divorce should become more difficult to obtain. Proponents of easy divorce point out that making divorce more difficult to obtain would prolong the distress of those in abusive relationships. Instead of making divorce more difficult to obtain, a number of social scientists have argued that new strategies for coping with divorce should be explored. These could include parenting coalitions, increased fathering, and other strategies to reduce the anxiety that divorce may create in children.

• Almost half of all marriages in any one year in the United States currently are remarriages. Remarriages are less stable than first marriages for whites. The reverse is the case for African Americans. Age, number of children, education, race, and ethnicity affect the likelihood of remarriage, but they affect men and women in different ways. Most couples who remarry do so only after cohabiting.

• Approximately 40 percent of children currently being born will spend some time in a stepfamily before they reach age 18. There are four types of stepfamilies with residential children that are formed either after divorce or widowhood: custodial mother-stepfather families, custodial father-stepmother families, dual stepparent families, and blended nuclear stepfamilies. In addition, there are two types of families with visiting stepchildren: non-custodial father-stepmother families and non-custodial mother-stepfather families.

• The social organization of stepfamilies tends to be different from traditional nuclear families. Typically, stepfamilies are characterized by complex social organization, vague boundaries that define who is in and outside the family, and vague social norms that specify what is expected of each family member. Stepfamilies tend to have low levels of cohesion and high levels of adaptability, which are functional for bi-nuclear families.

• Discipline in stepfamilies usually takes one of the following forms. The biological parent may be the disciplinarian. The parents may work together and prioritize their demands regarding the discipline of the children. The stepparent may participate in disciplining the child and remain firm until the child complies. The age of stepchildren influences the kind of relationship that develops between children and their stepparents.

• Approximately half of all children whose parents divorce and remarry will have a parent go through a second divorce. Explanations for redivorce focus on "kinds of people" who divorce and remarry and the family dynamics in stepfamilies. Redivorce creates issues of child support, child custody, and visitation between the stepparent and former spouse.

• Although the primary AIDS risk groups are still homosexual men, intravenous drug users, and partners of intravenous drug users, AIDS is becoming a concern of women, minorities, the poor, children of AIDS sufferers, and teenagers. Each of these groups has its own special problems related to AIDS. The number of women infected with HIV has increased rapidly over the past decade.

• Families of AIDS sufferers typically go through a stage of responses including shock and denial, anger, guilt and blame, fear, and social isolation. Unlike victims of other diseases, people with AIDS are likely to experience discrimination. The discrimination and social isolation experienced by AIDS sufferers generally adds to the hardships experienced by families of AIDS patients.

• A growing number of adult children are continuing to remain home living with their parents or return home after a divorce or unsuccessful career. Because the American family follows a neolocal residence pattern, this often creates strain for the parents. Factors that affect the parents' level of satisfaction with having an "unlaunched child" in the home include whether or not there are other children living there, the employment status of the adult child, and whether or not grandchildren are brought into the home.

• There are a number of characteristics that social scientists have found that make families strong and help family members cope with the stress of everyday life. These include: viewing love as multifaceted, keeping the sexual relationship satisfying, spending time together, sharing family responsibilities, using pregnancy as a bonding experience, using authoritative parenting, using assertive communication, resolving conflicts non-violently, and easing the divorce experience for children.

KEY TERMS

The following key terms are found in your textbook on the page number indicated in parentheses. In the space provided, write a brief definition of the key term. Then provide an example of the term, such as a culture in which the practice takes place, or people that you might know whose behavior illustrates the term. You could include issues that you might have read about in the news or in a book, or anything else that will illustrate the term and help you remember it. Include any comments from your class discussions or textbook that might help you remember and understand these key terms.

self-fulfilling prophecy (p. 444)

binuclear families (p. 446)

dual-stepparent families (p. 448)

vague boundaries (p. 450)

role ambiguity (p. 450)

cohesion (p. 450)

adaptability (p. 451)

redivorce (p. 453)

AIDS (p. 455)

HIV (p. 455)

____

____

____

unlaunched adult children (p. 462)

____

____

____

neolocal residence (p. 462)

____

____

____

parenting coalitions (p. 444)

____

____

____

NOTES:

PRACTICE TEST

Multiple Choice

1. In response to the economic and emotional disruption children experience during a divorce, many Americans:
   a) believe that divorce should be easier to obtain
   b) are questioning the advisability of easy divorce
   c) believe that parents should stay together no matter how bad their relationship is until the children are old enough to take care of themselves
   d) believe that the government should provide tax breaks for people who experience a divorce

2. Social scientists such as Arlene Skolnick believe that the best way to help alleviate the economic and emotional disruption that children may experience during a divorce is to:
   a) make divorce more difficult to obtain
   b) make divorce easier to obtain
   c) develop strategies for coping with divorce
   d) encourage parents to stay together for the sake of the children

3. The concept of parenting coalitions refers to:
   a) parents joining together behind the scenes to develop strategies to convince the children that the divorce is in their best interests
   b) community organizations designed to provide network support for divorced parents
   c) a joint custody situation in which the families in the households of the two divorced parents cooperate in child-rearing
   d) classes that the courts may require parents to attend after a divorce

4. That the high rate of divorce among adult children of divorce may be due to a self-fulfilling prophecy means that:
   a) the anxiety over the possibility of divorce for these children increases the probability that they will get divorced
   b) children whose parents are divorced are more likely to feel that divorce is a means of enhancing their self-esteem
   c) adult children of divorce are virtually pre-destined to get divorced themselves
   d) adult children of divorce are more likely to get divorced themselves because it is a means of identifying with their parents

5. Which of the following factors is not related to the likelihood of remarriage?
   a) political affiliation
   b) age
   c) race and ethnicity
   d) number of children

6. Of the following, who are least likely to remarry after divorce?
   a) middle-aged men without children
   b) women over age 40
   c) women over age 40 with children
   d) women under age 25 without children

7. Approximately what percent of children currently being born will spend some time in a stepfamily before they reach age 18?
   a) 10%
   b) 25%
   c) 40%
   d) 60%

8. What is the most common type of stepfamily with residential stepchildren?
   a) custodial mother-stepfather families
   b) custodial father-stepmother families
   c) dual-stepparent families
   d) blended nuclear and stepfamilies

9. The relationship between a child and stepfather tends to be most positive when:
   a) the stepparent does not act as a substitute for the biological father
   b) the biological father has frequent contact with the child
   c) the biological father and stepfather work together as co-fathers
   d) the stepparent becomes a substitute for the biological father

10. Which of the following statements about stepparents is true?
   a) stepmothers tend to have more positive relationships with their stepchildren than stepfathers
   b) stepfathers tend to have more positive relationships with their stepchildren than stepmothers
   c) stepmothers tend to have more positive relationships with their stepchildren than do the children's biological mother
   d) stepfathers tend to have more positive relationships with their stepchildren than do the children's biological father

11. As compared to traditional nuclear families, stepfamilies typically:
   a) are less complex with regard to interpersonal relationships
   b) have much more clear boundaries as to who is in the family and who is not
   c) have more clear norms and roles regarding behavior
   d) are more complex with regard to interpersonal relationships

12. A number of social science researchers have suggested that stepfamilies tend to function more smoothly if:
a) the bonds of connectedness are weaker
b) the bonds of connectedness are stronger
c) adaptability is low
d) cohesion is high

13. Which of the following groups has the lowest probability of redivorce?
a) women with college education
b) women without children from a previous marriage
c) men with post-graduate college training
d) men without children from a previous marriage

14. What is currently the fastest growing AIDS risk group?
a) homosexual men
b) intravenous drug users
c) heterosexual women partners of intravenous drug users
d) lesbian partners of intravenous drug users

15. Most women who have contracted AIDS are:
a) white, upper-middle class heterosexuals
b) African-American, upper-middle class heterosexuals
c) middle-income lesbians
d) low-income minorities

16. The highest rate of AIDS cases among women in the United States is found in:
a) Washington, D.C.
b) Florida
c) California
d) New York

17. Approximately what percent of African-Americans are infected with AIDS?
a) less than one percent
b) 5 percent
c) 10 percent
d) 20 percent

18. Why is AIDS often called the "grandmother's disease?"
a) because the incubation rate for AIDS is so long that people often do not emerge with full blown AIDS until they are well into middle age
b) because people who contract AIDS are often people who were teen parents and AIDS does not appear until their children are of child-bearing age themselves
c) because AIDS often attacks women in the prime of their childbearing years leaving motherless children to be raised by their grandparents
d) because contracting AIDS makes one age very rapidly

19. Which of the following responses to AIDS is/are likely to be experienced more by families of AIDS patients that by families of people with other terminal diseases?
a) shock and denial
b) anger
c) guilt and blame
d) social isolation and discrimination

20. A neolocal residence pattern means that:
a) young adults are expected to live near their parents
b) young adults are expected to take their parents in during their elderly years
c) young adults are expected to establish a residence separate from that of their parents
d) young adults are expected to enter a process of moving from a smaller to a larger home as their family develops

21. Approximately how many mid-life parents still have an adult child living in the home?
a) 10 percent
b) 25 percent
c) 45 percent
d) 65 percent

22. Which of the following is not a factor generally associated with the parents' level of satisfaction with having an unlaunched child living with them?
a) whether or not there are other children (under age eighteen) still living in the home
b) the gender of the unlaunched child
c) the employment status of the unlaunched child
d) whether or not grandchildren accompany the unlaunched child

23. Social scientists increasingly are recognizing that:
   a) the traditional nuclear family has proven itself to be the most stable family form
   b) two-earner families have better environments for raising children than the traditional single-earner family
   c) families in which there are androgynous gender roles in breadwinning, parenting, and maintaining a household are the most stable family form
   d) there is no single family form that is necessarily superior to other forms and many factors must be taken into consideration

24. The impact of divorce on children:
   a) is invariably negative
   b) is usually positive because the parents were not happy while together
   c) may be positive or negative, depending upon how the parents handle the divorce experience
   d) cannot be measured scientifically

25. The general trend in society with regard to family life is that:
   a) families are moving increasingly toward a single family form
   b) families are becoming more unified in their approaches to marital relationships and child-rearing
   c) families are becoming more complex and diverse
   d) families are declining in importance

NOTES:

PROJECTS

PROJECT 16. 1 Reflecting on the Resilience of Your Own Family

Throughout the text, Robin Wolf has emphasized the theme of family diversity. There is not one type of "normal" family. However, she did discuss various factors that lead to and are representative of healthy families. She closes the final chapter of her text with a discussion on efactors that are related to create resilient families. The objective of this project is to have you observe and reflect upon the resilience of your family. Hopefully, you can use this knowledge to help keep your current and future family resilient or, if necessary, to help pave the way for increasing the resilience of your family.

Journal instructions:

1. Re-read the section in Chapter 16 on resilient families. If you have not already done so, re-read the sections in the various chapters throughout the text that discuss each of these factors in depth.

2. In your journal, write each of the factors associated with resilient families at the top of separate pages. After you write down each factor, provide a brief discussion or summary of what Robin Wolf says about it. Allow around four or five pages in between each factor. For example, at the top of the first page write "viewing love as multifaceted," summarize Robin Wolf's comments on what this means and how it leads to resiliency in families, and then leave around four or five blank pages. Do this for each factor that Wolf says leads to resilient families.

3. For one to two weeks, keep a detailed daily record of how each factor is demonstrated by your family. If you are away from home and not able to observe your family on a daily basis, set aside one hour each day to reflect on how the factors in your family that help to create resilience. Write about the resiliency factors, along with the dates, under the respective headings that you provided in your journal. Provide a brief description of what occurred and how it represents the resiliency factor. For example, note how love is demonstrated in various ways, how family members spend time together, how responsibilities are shared, how positive forms of communication and parenting take place, and so on. Be as descriptive and as thorough as possible.

4. In addition to identifying the factors in your family that help to create resilience, for one to two weeks keep a detailed record of events in which a resiliency factor could have been created or improved. As above, if you are unable to observe your family directly, set aside one hour each day to reflect on the ways in which resiliency in your family can be improved. For example, you may

observe (or reflect on) situations in which a different type of communication might have been used, an opportunity in which love could have been expressed, an opportunity in which family members could have spent more time together, and so on. Describe as many opportunities as possible in which you can find ways to improve family resilience.

Option: essay
Write an essay (around five pages, typed) in which you discuss the extent to which your family is resilient and what can be done to improve the resilience of your family based upon the factors you reflected upon in your journal.

Option: bibliography
Select two or three of the factors that lead to resilience that you observed that your family has or does not have. Create a bibliography of fifteen to twenty articles and books that discuss these factors. For example, you might look for articles on the effects of divorce on children, communication in families, conflict resolution, and so on. Be sure that at least half of your sources are from social science journals or are books written by social scientists. Type your bibliography following the bibliographic format found in the social science journals or in your textbook.

Option: research paper
Write a paper (seven to nine pages, typed) in which you discuss what you think are the two or three most important factors that create resilience in families. Integrate material from the observations of your own family and from at least five of the items from the bibliography you developed (above). Be sure to provide proper documentation throughout your paper and include a reference page.

Suggestion: If you discussed in your journal the factors that help to make your family resilient, you might use your family, then, to illustrate how various factors help to create resilient families. Or you can use ideas found in items from your bibliography to help explain why your family is resilient. On the other hand, if you discussed in your journal things that need improving in your family to help make it more resilient, you again might use your family as an example of how the factors you selected could benefit families. Or you can use ideas found in items from your bibliography to help explain why your family is not resilient.

NOTES:

ANSWER KEY TO PRACTICE TESTS

CHAPTER 1

1. c
2. b
3. a
4. c
5. b
6. b
7. d
8. d
9. d
10. d
11. b
12. a
13. c
14. b
15. d
16. a
17. c
18. a
19. b
20. b

CHAPTER 2

1. d
2. c
3. a
4. b
5. c
6. b
7. a
8. b
9. c
10. c
11. d
12. a
13. b
14. a
15. b
16. a
17. d
18. b
19. a
20. b
21. c
22. d
23. a
24. d
25. a
26. d
27. c
28. c
29. a
30. d

CHAPTER 3

1. c
2. a
3. b
4. d
5. a
6. c
7. b
8. b
9. d
10. a
11. b
12. a
13. c
14. b
15. c
16. d
17. a
18. a
19. b
20. c

CHAPTER 4

1. b
2. a
3. d
4. b
5. c
6. d
7. c
8. d
9. b
10. d
11. d
12. b
13. a
14. d.
15. c
16. c
17. b
18. a
19. a
20. c
21. d
22. b
23. b
24. a
25. c
26. a
27. d
28. d
29. c
30. b

CHAPTER 5

1. b
2. a
3. c
4. b
5. c
6. a
7. c
8. c
9. c
10. d
11. b
12. c
13. b
14. d
15. a
16. d
17. c
18. a
19. c
20. d

CHAPTER 6

1. d
2. a
3. b
4. c
5. b
6. d
7. d
8. a
9. c
10. d
11. b
12. b
13. c
14. d
15. c
16. b
17. d
18. b
19. a
20. c
21. b
22. b
23. b
24. b
25. c

CHAPTER 7

1. c
2. c
3. a
4. b
5. b
6. d
7. c
8. d
9. c
10. d
11. a
12. a
13. c
14. b
15. d
16. b
17. a
18. b
19. a
20. d

CHAPTER 8

1. b
2. c
3. c
4. d
5. a
6. a
7. c
8. b
9. b
10. c
11. d
12. a
13. c
14. a
15. c
16. d
17. b
18. b
19. a
20. a

CHAPTER 9

1. b
2. c
3. b
4. d
5. a
6. c
7. b
8. c
9. c
10. c
11. d
12. a
13. a
14. b
15. c
16. b
17. d
18. c
19. b
20. a

CHAPTER 10

1. a
2. a
3. c
4. b
5. d
6. d
7. a
8. b
9. a
10. d
11. c
12. c
13. b
14. a
15. c
16. a
17. d
18. c
19. b
20. a
21. b
22. b
23. a
24. d
25. d

CHAPTER 11

1. c
2. a
3. a
4. d
5. b
6. a
7. a
8. a
9. b
10. a
11. c
12. c
13. d
14. b
15. b
16. d
17. b
18. c
19. a
20. c
21. a
22. d
23. d
24. d
25. c
26. b
27. b
28. a
29. a
30. b

CHAPTER 12

1. b
2. b
3. b
4. c
5. c
6. c
7. a
8. b
9. a
10. a
11. d
12. c
13. b
14. b
15. a
16. c
17. a
18. d
19. a
20. b
21. c
22. b
23. d
24. a
25. c

CHAPTER 13

1. a
2. b
3. d
4. a
5. b
6. c
7. b
8. d
9. a
10. a
11. b
12. a
13. a
14. b
15. c
16. d
17. a
18. c
19. a
20. b
21. c
22. c
23. d
24. a
25. a

CHAPTER 14

1. b
2. b
3. c
4. a
5. b
6. d
7. c
8. d
9. a
10. b
11. d
12. a
13. c
14. c
15. a
16. d
17. d
18. d
19. c
20. a
21. d
22. a
23. a
24. c
25. b

CHAPTER 15

1. b
2. d
3. a
4. c
5. c
6. b
7. a
8. c
9. b
10. b
11. a
12. a
13. d
14. c
15. a
16. c
17. c
18. d
19. d
20. d
21. a
22. b
23. d
24. c
25. d

CHAPTER 16

1. b
2. c
3. c
4. a
5. a
6. c
7. c
8. a
9. d
10. b
11. d
12. a
13. c
14. c
15. d
16. d
17. a
18. c
19. d
20. c
21. c
22. b
23. d
24. c
25. c